AN ADIRONDACK SAMPLER
Day Hikes for All Seasons

by Bruce Wadsworth

Mountain Club

CONSERVATION · EDUCATION · RECREATION

ADIRONDACK MOUNTAIN CLUB
Lake George, New York

Third Edition

Published by The Adirondack Mountain Club, Inc.
RR3, Box 3055, Lake George, New York 12845-9523

Library of Congress Cataloging-in-Publications Data

Wadsworth, Bruce.
   An Adirondack Sampler:
      Day Hikes For All Seasons/by Bruce Wadsworth - - 3rd ed.
   Includes index.
   ISBN 0-935272-60-7
   1. Hiking - - New York (State) - - Adirondack Mountains - -
            Guide-books.
   2. Adirondack Mountains (N.Y.) - - Description and travel - -
            Guide-books.
I. Title.
GV199.42.N652A348   1991   91-36397
917.47'5—dc20   CIP

Third edition, 1992
Printed and bound in the United States of America

Cover design: The Design Function
Photo acknowledgments: p. 33, Lawrence King; p. 70, Robin Brown;
p. 80, Ralph Geiser; pp. 59 and 66 courtesy of the Adirondack Museum.
All other photographs, sketches, and maps contributed by the author.

Contents

Rondaxe (Bald) Mountain Fire Tower, 1930

Dedication

This guidebook is dedicated to the fire tower observers of the Adirondack Park. Many trails used by the hiker today exist only because they lead, or once led, to a tower manned by these memorable men and women. The strong, positive feelings of many New Yorkers for their Adirondacks must, like mine, be partly due to happy memories of times spent with fire observers on mountain tops.

Fire observers have guarded our forests since 1912, when the first fire towers were authorized. Today, air surveillance and other means of fire detection have reduced, and are continuing to reduce, their numbers. One of the saddest parts about writing this book was finding so many closed towers and foundations of removed towers on mountain peaks.

Time stands still for no one, but let us not forget the dedication and lonely service of the fire observers. These philosophers and raconteurs of the peaks did much to add color and character to the mountain experiences of those of us who were privileged to share their towers.

Acknowledgments

It's hard to believe this guide has been introducing hiking trails of the Adirondacks to recreationists since 1979. At the time of its inception, there was a concentration of hiking in the High Peaks that was detrimental both to the ecology of the area and to the hikers' maximum enjoyment of the out-of-doors. *An Adirondack Sampler,* followed by ADK's Forest Preserve Series of trail guides, helped disperse the hiking public to the whole of the Adirondack Park and relieve traffic in the High Peaks Region.

Several changes have occurred during this time, and many people have assisted me in the task of keeping the book current. Besides the individuals acknowledged in the first two editions, others must be mentioned as this latest edition comes to print.

Users of earlier editions have been most kind in providing me with updates whenever trail changes have been noted. Forest rangers unfailingly lent insight; conversations with them are always rewarding.

David MacPherson introduced me to Gilligan Mt. while on a trail-clearing trip. When the removal of the fire tower from Boreas Mt. also removed the possibility of a good view, Gilligan Mt. was substituted.

As has been the case for many years, Carmen Elliott continued on the production end to make the manuscript into an actual book. Her ideas and professional direction have been instrumental in this venture's success.

Finally, thanks must be given to my wife, Betty, who is almost always with me as I hike these trails.

Introduction

"It's a great thing these days to leave civilization for awhile."

Robert Marshall, 1937

An Adirondack Sampler was written as an introduction to that vast and marvelous region called the Adirondacks. It invites you to visit the trails, streams, and mountains of the largest park in the contiguous United States and will guide you into some of the nicest places in the Adirondacks reachable on foot.

The *Sampler* was planned for the single-day forest traveler; most of the hikes can be completed in six hours or less. It is for those who are just beginning the adventure of hiking as well as for those who have traveled the more rugged high peaks and are now seeking less challenging, but just as enjoyable, journeys. It is ideal for family outings. The winter hiker, especially the snowshoer, will find the *Sampler* a welcome companion.

This guidebook contains hikes in all regions of the Adirondack Park. It is not necessary, or even desirable, to begin one's climbing experience in the high peaks around Mt. Marcy. Too often the neophyte in the High Peaks lacks either the stamina or the skills — or both — needed to enjoy such trips. The hikes described here will enable the beginner to gain the know-how necessary for longer excursions while fully enjoying the forest experience.

The *Sampler* is for the many day hikers who simply want to enjoy the out-of-doors on a fine weekend. For you, the Adirondacks can be summed up by the deer that magically appears at lakeside at day's end, by a cascading brook in springtime, by the falling leaves of autumn hardwoods. For you, a quiet place with a beautiful view encourages contemplation; a rippling stream evokes pleasant thoughts. Not for you a crowded trail to Mt. Marcy.

The Adirondacks are full of rippling streams, quiet ponds, and hundreds of seldom-trod trails. Dozens of mountains patiently await the occasional visitor Go and visit them. One of them is sure to become your own special place.

WHAT DO YOU NEED?

The otherwise interested hiker is often bewildered by the wide assortment of equipment available on the market today. To be discouraged for this reason would be a great mistake. First, day hikes are not lengthy expeditions. Second, while equipment should be sturdy and dependable, it doesn't have to be expensive. Third, though there are factors that must be addressed before plunging into the forest, they are relatively few in number: comfort, adaptability to changing conditions, health, safety, and personal interests. Most people will find they already have several of the items needed for hiking. Purchase equipment that will satisfy *your* needs.

Comfort. Since your feet are going to get you there, treat them kindly. Generally, the steeper the trail or the heavier the climber, the more rugged should be the footwear. Acceptable footwear should fit well, be sturdy, provide ankle support, and have good traction. Shoes or boots should be well broken in. For most of the hikes in this book, sneakers or work shoes will be quite adequate. Light or medium-weight hiking boots would be nicer to have, though. Sneakers may be fine on a flat, dry trail of a short distance, but they can become mighty uncomfortable on a muddy mountain trail that suddenly fills up with water during an unexpected deluge. Many hikers wear an outer pair of heavy woolen socks and a lighter pair of socks under them to reduce friction. Rest occasionally so your feet can cool off. Otherwise, they may present you with a blister to remind you to be more concerned with their welfare.

In everyday life most of us don't think much about walking. We get up from the table and walk to the living room, car, or kitchen. The act is over after a dozen or so steps. Hiking is considerably different. Besides having proper footwear, it helps a great deal to have your hands free. You don't mind carrying the picnic basket from the table to the car, but don't try to carry one five miles up a mountain. Put your food, sweater, and other gear in a pack of some sort. For a short trip this may be a travel bag over the shoulder. Eventually, however, you'll want a day pack. The cost, quality, and type depends upon your needs and your body build. Size can only be determined after you know what must be carried. Late fall and winter hiking require extra space for supplemental clothing. Many packs are compressible so that size can be altered. Generally, soft packs rather than external frame packs are more comfortable for day hikes. Some light internal frame packs are also excellent. Fifteen or twenty pounds are as much as a person can easily tote all day. Carry less if possible. Make sure the pack stitching is good and that stress points are double-stitched. Try on several styles to find which type feels comfortable on your back. An "occasional" hiker doesn't need the same quality gear as the "every weekend" hiker whose gear will get more wear and tear. Cost generally varies with quality.

Adaptability to Changing Conditions. Anyone who has spent much time in the Adirondacks has heard the old adage, "If you don't like the present weather, wait around another ten minutes and it'll change." Even when the weather doesn't change, the hiker will find it cooler in the forest than out in the meadow sun. The temperature drops and winds increase as elevation is gained. On the driest of days you'll still get soaked if you slip while crossing a stream. It is only good sense to prepare for the likely, but it is prudent to prepare for the unlikely as well.

One of the most simple, yet practical, items for adaptability is the hat. It protects you from the sun, rain, and insects. In cooler weather a wool cap will keep you warm even when wet. Wet, it will help cool you on a hot day. In the rain, its brim is a blessing. (Put some insect repellent around the brim and watch those pesky flies disappear.) Upwards to a third of your body heat can be controlled through your head. Getting warm after climbing awhile? Take your hat off. Getting cold? Put one on.

Make your equipment serve many functions. You may use a poncho to help keep you warm or protect you from the wind as well as to stay dry in the rain. Those extra socks you were wise enough to carry make pretty good mittens on a chilly day. A hood is desirable on that poncho or jacket. *The key to heat control is layering. Avoid perspiration.* Start with that golf jacket or light wool shirt you have in the closet. Consider the number of combinations a vest and rain jacket can offer. Carry items that can be taken off or added easily and make the adjustment as soon as your body indicates a change is needed. That heavy parka may be great for sitting in a cold stadium, but don't try to climb a mountain in one.

One more word is needed. The word is *hypothermia.* Briefly, hypothermia is a condition where heat loss exceeds the capability of the body to replace it. Body temperature decreases and death can result.

For this to happen, the air temperature need not be frigid. A high wind can quickly strip body heat away. Avoid cottons, which wick water and cause body heat loss. Use synthetics in the summer and wool in the winter. Avoid soaking your clothing with body perspiration. Remember the concept of clothing layering.

Should you or a companion find that gloves or other clothing items are being lost on the trail, stumbling is occurring while walking, shivering can't be controlled, thinking is difficult, or unusual responses occur when speaking, act without delay. Get hot food and drink into the person. High-energy, quickly digested food should be used. Get the person warmed in any manner possible.

Every hiker should be familiar with the symptoms of hypothermia and what remedial action to take to prevent it. Contact the Adirondack Mountain Club for more information.

Health. The forest is not the same as home. Whenever a person's environment is changed, health considerations should be examined.

Get a good night's rest before setting out on your trip. Follow that up with a good, high-energy breakfast so you'll maintain your stamina after a few hours of walking. Many hikers find it better to nibble food all through the day rather than have a single large midday meal. Hard candies, nuts, raisins and other dried fruits, sunflower seeds, granola, coconut, dried cereal, chocolate, and other readily available supermarket items make good trail food (gorp). Semi-sweet chocolate won't melt in hot weather. A fresh orange is great to have along. Avoid things that require cooking, or you'll be bogged down with pots, pans, and a sore back.

You'll drink more water than normal when you hike. Take a filled canteen or plastic jug with you. (Unfortunately, no water source on or off the trail can be considered safe to drink due to the prevalence of the parasite *Giardia lamblia*. Carry water purification tablets in case of emergency.) Carry extra food. And carry those wrappers and containers out with you.

It is often said that God's only mistake was creating the black fly. Spring hiking calls for a suitable insect repellent. The best ones all have the active ingredient N, N-diethyl-meta-toluamide. By mid-July you may be tempted to leave repellents at home, but don't do it. It's a very small item to carry for the relief provided when needed.

Carry a first-aid kit. It should contain an assortment of bandaids, salves, small bandages, and a small pair of scissors. An Ace bandage is nice to have if an ankle is turned. In extremely warm weather salt tablets may be needed.

Should you feel a tender spot developing on your foot, care for it immediately before it becomes a blister. Moleskin patches are handy for this. Cut a small hole in the center of the patch a little larger than the sore spot. Place the patch on the skin with the hole over the tender spot. The raised patch then keeps the boot from irritating it more.

Don't forget toilet tissue. While many hiking areas have privies at campsites along the trails, don't count on one being present when you need one. Leave the trail, select an area having soft earth, and make a small hole 6-8 inches deep. Cover it with leaf litter before leaving it. Nature will take care of the rest. Be sure to avoid areas which are near waterways.

Safety. Emergencies do occur, but their intensity may be greatly minimized if you are prepared for them. A few basic items can make the difference between inconvenience and disaster. Do not expect someone to appear simply because help is needed. Even if you were sensible enough to tell a neighbor or friend of your intended route of travel and your expected return time, help should not be expected for several hours.

Although it may appear difficult to become lost on the trails found in this guidebook, carry it with you anyway. It has information that will help you gain insight about your trip. In some cases maps have been included with the trail descriptions. As you take your rest breaks, open your guidebook and read from it. If you have a topographical map, ori-

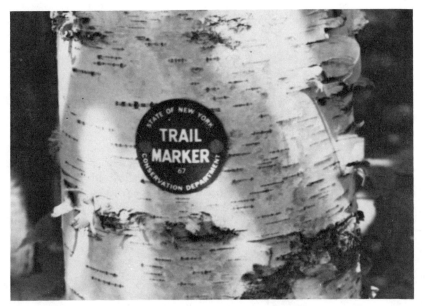

Typical trail marker

ent yourself and identify points of interest that are in view. Hiking is much more than simply getting from here to there. Awaken your senses to your environment. Learn more of your heritage. Become an integral part of your surroundings.

The trails in this guide are, for the most part, well marked, but you should always take a compass along. Check your compass direction before you begin your trip so you'll know which way to head should you become temporarily "misplaced." Take the time to become familiar with your compass *before* you need it.

Be sure to take plenty of dry matches. A candle greatly facilitates starting a fire in wet weather. If a fire is needed, build it on a rock base to prevent starting a ground fire in organic duff.

Every person in your group should carry a whistle. A lost child can panic. Teach him or her to sit down and use that whistle if separated from the party. The whistle can also be used to scare away a menacing animal. It's much safer than throwing things at it, which might cause it to attack you.

Time passes quickly when you're enjoying yourself. To avoid a return trip in the dark, do two things. Carry a watch, and carry a flashlight. Keep track of the time it takes you to cover different sections of your route and allow ample time to be off the trail before dark. Rely on the flashlight only for emergency use.

A small jackknife will have a multitude of uses. Don't wear one of those huge belt knives unless you're planning to skin a buffalo. A small jackknife with a couple different-sized blades will fill the bill.

Many hikers carry a space blanket. They are light, small, and can be very useful if you get caught out overnight. They can be extremely important if a person is seriously injured and must be kept warm.

Don't start filling your pockets with all these little items. Walking will be most unpleasant. Instead, make a ditty bag out of some scrap material and attach a drawstring to close it. Throw all the loose items into the little sack and dump it into the bottom of your pack. You'll know where everything is and packing becomes a cinch.

Personal Interests. Plan to enjoy yourself. What do you like to do? Take a camera if you like photography. Perhaps a field identification guide of flowers, birds, or animal tracks will make your trip more fun. A small pair of binoculars can make a view outstanding. Maybe you would just like to read a novel and while away the time. Whatever it is, tuck it into your pack and have a good time.

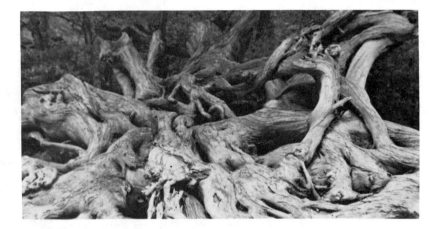

Checklist of Hiking Equipment

Day Pack
Compass
Food and Water
Jackknife
Candle
Insect Repellent
Salt Tablets
Wool Sweater/Shirt
Hat
Watch
Toilet Tissue
Ditty Bag

Map (Guidebook)
Canteen
Flashlight
Matches
First-aid Kit
Water Purification Tablets
Jacket with Hood
Poncho or Other Rain Gear
Extra Socks
Whistle
Space Blanket
Personal Interest Items

TRIP DIFFICULTY

Each hike description in this guidebook begins with a basic listing of information that will enable you to approximate the hike's difficulty. Distances and elevations do not require evaluation except to determine if the trips are within your capability. The data are quite accurate. Your judgment must be used to make best use of some of the other information.

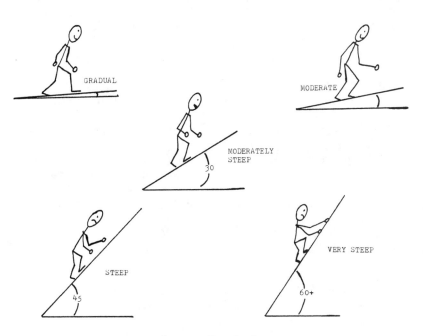

Steepness Standards

Times for round trips are generally conservative. Some people walk faster than others, and even the same person may push on rapidly when a storm beckons overhead but will tarry while looking at wildflowers on a warm spring day. Are you in good physical condition? Do you have a small child along with you who may have to be carried from time to time? These are variables that must be considered. After a trip or two you should be able to compare travel times on past outings and make adjustments from the given travel times to determine the travel times that best fit your style of hiking.

What is "steep" to one person is "easy" to another. No two people seem to evaluate trail difficulty in the same manner. In the trail descriptions an attempt has been made to standardize the use of terms relating to steepness. Five terms are used: gradual, moderate, moderately steep, steep, and very steep. The terms are based upon relative grade, not on ease of travel. How "easy" the grades will seem to you depends upon your physical condition, experience, and mental outlook.

DISTANCE AND ELEVATION

New topographic maps are being printed in metric units, while most of the maps currently in use have the English units. Therefore, distances and elevations have been expressed both in English and metric units. Metric units are placed in parentheses following the English units. The abbreviation *m* means meters in the metric system; *km* means kilometers. One kilometer equals one thousand meters. Indicated distances have been kept to a minimum in this book. Most trips are fairly short and the intermediate distances are not really essential for following the route.

MAPS

Maps are used to help you locate and follow several of the trails described in this book. These maps often include other trails not described in this book but that may be of interest to you. Each described trail includes the topographical map quadrangles on which the trail is located. These quadrangles are 15-minute maps unless otherwise indicated.

In mapping, the term *minute* is used to represent an angle measurement. There are 60 minutes in 1 degree. There are 360 degrees in the circle encompassing the earth. A 15-minute map shows the ground area which represents 15 minutes of longitude x 15 minutes of latitude. In the Adirondacks, a 15-minute map represents a ground distance of about 12.5 mi. (20 km) in an east-west direction and about 17.5 mi. (28 km) in a north-south direction. In some cases, 7.5-minute maps are available. Such maps represent one-fourth the ground area and one-half the distances of the 15-minute map in each direction. They permit greater detail since less ground area is represented on the same size paper used for the 15-minute map. Because they are not uniformly available for Adirondack areas, 7.5-minute quadrangles have not been listed in this book.

Since 1978, a third type of map has been introduced. This is a 7.5-minute x 15-minute quadrangle using metric units. In preparation for the 1980 Olympic Games at Lake Placid, the United States Geological Survey (USGS) made the first maps in the United States for the Adirondack region. In effect, it is like putting two 7.5-minute maps side by side. Since the actual size of the map sheet is large compared to the 15-minute map and the map scale is much larger than a 15-minute map, great detail can be shown with this map. It is expected that these maps will be the predominantly used maps of the future.

For each hike described in this book, the 15-minute quadrangle and the metric quadrangle (if available) are listed.

TRAIL MANNERS

Remember that you are a visitor in a place of natural beauty. What you have come to see, others will come after you to see. The saying, "Take only pictures, leave only footprints," is an excellent motto to follow. Many hikers habitually carry litter bags and clear trails as they return after a trip. There are signs that the modern hiker is becoming more conscious of his personal obligation to maintain his natural surroundings. Set a good example.

Many trails are partially or totally on private lands. The continued use of these lands by the hiking public is often directly related to how the public uses that land. The trails and places of beauty must be kept litter-free and in good condition. Do your part. If you carry it in, carry it out. When possible, also be willing to carry out litter left by others.

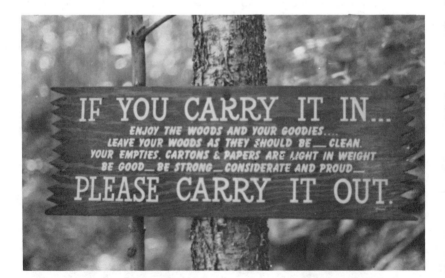

CAMPFIRES

There is a growing ethic that open fires should not be built in the wild except in those areas specifically established for that purpose. Lean-tos normally have fireplaces, as do certain camping areas. Remember that the Forest Preserve land is to be "forever wild." This means that no standing trees may be legally cut. Use dead and down wood only. While everyone enjoys a campfire at night, you'll find that camp cooking will be cleaner, faster, and can be done safely in more places if a small portable camper's stove is carried with you on overnight trips.

WINTER HIKING

Winter hiking, snowshoeing, and cross-country skiing are all becoming very popular. Many of the trips included in this guidebook are excellent for these activities.

One must keep in mind that hiking in winter is far different from summer hiking. Travel times will be much longer. Energy demands are greater. Clothing requirements are more strict. Tolerances for error are much less. Winter in the woods is beautiful, but do not take preparation for even an afternoon's outing lightly. Weather conditions in the Adirondacks can be as severe as those found anywhere else on this earth. Wet rains and freezing winds can be disastrous. Whiteouts can turn a short mountain climb into an overnight struggle for survival.

The novice should gain winter experience in organized groups such as the chapters of the Adirondack Mountain Club and with knowledgeable individuals. Do not go out alone in the winter. It is recommended, in summer or winter, to have at least four members in your group as a minimum for safety. In case of injury this permits one person to remain with the injured party while the other two go for help.

FIRE TOWERS

Many trails described in this guidebook originally were built to lead to summit fire towers. Today, you will probably find the tower either unmanned or gone. A word of caution about unmanned fire towers: Closed

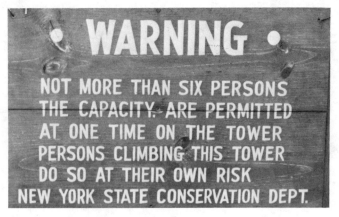

fire towers generally are not well maintained and may be in disrepair. They should be considered dangerous. If you should decide to climb one for a better view, use extreme care.

TRAVEL SAFETY

The hiker is reminded that trail conditions vary through time. Rains make some areas very slippery. Spring meltwaters can wash out bridges.

While trails are generally in good repair, manpower for trail maintenance is a continuing problem. It behooves the hiker to use common sense and reasonable precautions if unusual conditions are encountered.

TRAIL CORRECTIONS

Trail changes are inevitable. It would be greatly appreciated if hikers would notify the Adirondack Mountain Club when such changes are found. In this way, future guidebook editions can be updated and corrected. Send any such information to the Adirondack Mountain Club, R.R. 3, Box 3055, Lake George, NY 12845-9523.

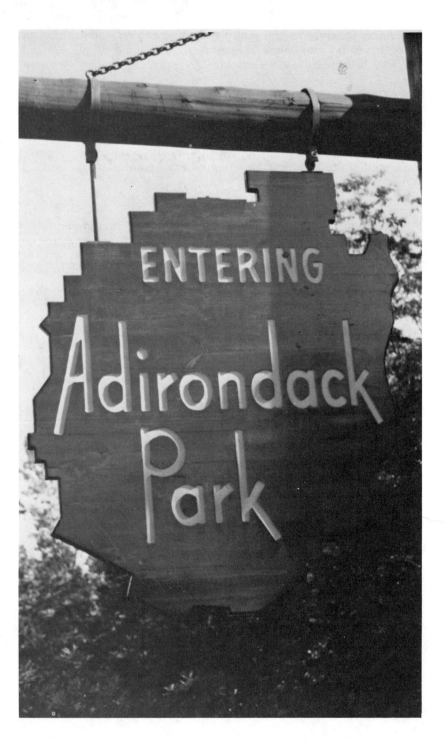

The Adirondacks

Some particular place generally comes to mind when a person thinks about "the Adirondacks." It may be a summer camp, a favorite hiking trail, or the special view from a certain mountain top. Whatever or wherever it may be, it is almost always a relatively small geographical area with which the individual has developed intimacy. Each person creates for himself a private concept of what constitutes the "Adirondacks."

Let's take a look at the whole of the Adirondack Park for a moment. It is as large as the state of Connecticut and as varied as the people who live within it. It is an Adirondacks that few people seem to know a great deal about, even though they may have gone to "their" Adirondacks for many years.

We can broadly divide the Adirondacks into two sections. The Mountain Belt consists of five parallel ranges running southwestward from Lake Champlain. They are the Luzerne Range, Kayaderosseras Range, Schroon Range, Boquet Range, and the Adirondack Range. The second great division is the Lake Region to the west of the Mountain Belt. This comparatively flat country is covered with long chains of lakes separated by rolling forests.

The Adirondacks are part of the vast Canadian Shield and are very old. Over a billion years ago, intrusions far beneath the surface of the earth melted and forced their way from Canada into the heart of this region. Then, swelling upward like a gigantic blister, the doming process which culminated in today's high peaks slowly began.

Anorthosite rock formed under these conditions. This grey-blue plagioclase feldspar with book lenses of mica is readily found throughout this area. Away from the center, more moderate forces changed the existing rock less. Around this core, gneisses are found. The alternation of different colored bands of minerals often makes them obvious to those who are looking for them. Since these geological activities changed the original rock, the rocks are said to be metamorphic.

Most metamorphic rock is more dense than the original rock from which it formed. It has experienced so much pressure that water can no longer penetrate it. Thus the winter meltwaters must drain off the surface rather than become subsurface groundwater.

Long Lake, Indian Lake, and Lake George are just a few examples of places where extensive breaks in the rock, called faults, have filled with water. The sharply angular turns that characterize so many Adirondack streams show where other rock breaks, called joint patterns, are followed by runoff waters. It seems as though every depression forms a pond.

During its most recent geological history, the Ice Age sculptured this land. Rounding off mountain tops and filling in valleys, glaciers created still more lakes. Isolated blocks of ice sank into the ground and then melted. Kettlehole lakes, such as Heart Lake, resulted from this process. Where no drainage was possible from a depression, bogs formed. Receding glaciers frequently built a series of natural dams called moraines.

Chains of lakes, so common in the Adirondacks, formed behind these moraines.

Glacial erratic, Azure Mountain

Hence, the stage upon which the dynamic drama of life in the Adirondacks is played has three principal parts. The hard platform floor keeps the waters on or near the land surface. The geological processes which made this region have provided channels through which the waters may drain off. The last Ice Age made this drainage difficult, so much water remains.

The hard metamorphic rock breaks down slowly. The soils are shallow because of this. As grades increase on mountainsides, the effects of erosion become more pronounced. Soil thickness becomes very thin. Heavy rains may saturate this soil. Landslides may then carry soil, trees, and everything else into the valleys.

It is on this thin mountain soil that man builds his trails. Newcomers frequently wonder why these trails often seem to go up stream beds. They don't realize that these "trail" streams came *after* man, not before him. His relentless walking has broken the soil and gravity has carried it away. Over the years the trails have become the low spots into which the surrounding waters descended. There is a lesson to be learned here. Always walk on rock where possible. Don't start that first depression that may become a stream bed in twenty years.

The kinds of plant life found in the Adirondacks are many. While the local environment will determine exactly which species will be found in a given area, Adirondack vegetation can be broadly grouped into five categories, referred to as site types: white pine, spruce swamp forest, mixed wood, hardwoods, and upper spruce slope sites. Characterized by a few readily identified trees, these sites tend to have specialized wildlife communities of plants and animals.

A trail stream

The white pine site type is generally found on sandy plains areas. It predominates from Lake Champlain to Glens Falls. White pines and other trees which have deep tap roots are most common. Mineral soils restrict what can survive there.

The spruce swamp site type is found wherever peaty or mucky soils occur in wet areas. If the swampy area has stagnant water, black spruces will be most common. If the water can flow easily, red spruce and balsam firs will be dominant.

The mixed woods begin above the swampy zones. The term "mixed woods" refers to the fact that both softwood and hardwood trees are found growing together in the same area. Soils are better and are slightly drier. Red maple, yellow birch, and hemlocks are most common. The softwoods decrease as elevations increase. The upper limit of this site type is reached where beeches begin to be seen.

Drainage is ideal on the lower mountain slopes. This is where the hardwood site type is found. The soils are very productive here. The primary trees are sugar maples and beech. However, yellow birch, black cherry, white ash, and other trees are found in lesser numbers.

21

Finally, at about 2500 ft. (765 m), the upper spruce slope site type begins. The red spruce and balsam fir again dominate. Tree size decreases as elevation increases. A timber line is reached if the mountain is high enough. The paper birch and mountain ash are the only hardwoods found in this site type, and they'll only be found at the lower limits of elevation.

Learn to identify these few trees and you'll better appreciate the forest you're traveling through on your outings. It's contagious. You'll soon be wondering why the ferns in the spruce swamp are different from those of the hardwoods. Why do the spring flowers linger longer on the trail edges than deeper in the forest? You'll begin to notice that bird species change as elevation and tree types change. Subtle but powerful biological interactions are set into motion by slight environmental variances. As you begin to notice them, your day's hiking destination won't seem quite as important. Each step will bring new opportunities for discovery.

What might you discover? One of the world's great moss collections is found in the Adirondacks clinging to wet cliffs and ledges. You might notice the great long, winding, glacial ridges called eskers. Huge white pines are often found growing on them. In the acidic bogs you may discover delicate sundew plants or thick waxy pitcher plants. Trees can also tell you much. The gradual reddening of the birch bark as you gain elevation gives clues as to how far you have yet to climb. When the hardwoods blend into the red spruce and balsam fir, you'll know that you're getting along on your climb. Paper birches at high elevations are signs of past forest fires. Mixed woods tell you how long it has been since the last lumbering. Why is it that the hemlocks, so common around Lake George, are found only in wind-protected vales in the high peaks?

Everything you see in the Adirondacks has an interesting history. Varying physical factors combine to form distinctive local environments. Organisms must adapt to these environments or perish. Everything affects everything else. Remember that you also affect everything else.

Think of the whole of the Adirondacks as you seek out the charms of the special places that will become "your" Adirondacks. Take time to observe that which surrounds you. Learn the story it has to tell. It is the gift of the ages, and it began long before Man appeared to sing its praises.

Hardwood site, Snowy Mountain

Adirondak Loj, Heart Lake

The Adirondack Mountain Club (ADK)

The Adirondack Mountain Club (ADK) is a nonprofit conservation, education, and recreation organization founded in 1922 for the purpose of protecting and enjoying the Forest Preserve of New York State. Organized into 28 chapters in four states, the Club's 15,000 members find experienced and knowledgeable persons on a local level to share common interests and concerns and almost any desired outdoor activity: hiking, backpacking, camping, canoeing, skiing, snowshoeing, and winter mountaineering. Its members also enjoy All-Club Outings and extended trips throughout the world.

ADK publishes guidebooks, maps, and other books relating to the natural and social history of the Adirondacks. It also publishes educational brochures, a quarterly newsletter, and a magazine, *Adirondac*. Chapters publish their own newsletters as well, listing the hike schedules, monthly programs, and special activities of their local groups.

The Club sponsors outdoor skills workshops and natural history and educational programs promoting the appreciation and careful use of New York's wild lands. Club volunteers and a professional trail crew carry out trail maintenance throughout the High Peaks Region (some chapters also assume trail responsibility for areas outside the region) and administration of the Summit Stewards program, which seeks to educate the public about the fragile arctic/ alpine plans that grow on our highest peaks.

ADK operates two mountain lodges that serve as educational and recreational centers for Club members and the general public. Adirondak Loj, open all year, is a rustic, historic lodge eight miles south of Lake Placid on Heart Lake, on the site of Henry Van Hoevenberg's original turn-of-the-century log hotel. Loj accommodations include private and bunk rooms for forty-six persons. A separate rental cabin is available for groups of up to sixteen persons. Hearty meals are served family-style in the dining room. A lounge with fireplace offers a congenial atmosphere for after-dinner activities.

The Loj campgrounds, also open year round, have thirteen lean-tos and thirty-seven campsites. All lean-tos and campsites are open for winter camping, but sites for trailers and campers are usually inaccessible during snow months. The Club's High Peaks Information Center (HPIC) houses a large public room with educational displays, the latest backcountry information, and restrooms with hot showers. Its trading post offers last-minute camping and skiing supplies, trail snacks, and Adirondack-oriented publications.

In summer, a resident naturalist conducts seminars and programs and maintains a small nature museum. An outdoor amphitheater and several nature trails round out the Loj offerings. Ski and snowshoe rentals, guided tours, and skills instruction are available in the winter.

The Club also operates Johns Brook Lodge (JBL), a simple and informal complex 3½ miles by foot from the trailhead near Keene Valley. JBL provides an ideal base for hiking the Adirondack High Peaks Region. The main lodge is fully staffed from late June through Labor Day and can be used on a caretaker basis into October. The two out-buildings, Camp Peggy O'Brien and Grace Camp, have simple facilities where campers may cook their own meals and sleep in snug rooms year round. Campers using these facilities must supply their own sleeping equipment and pack in all necessary food and supplies. There are also three lean-tos available by reservation.

Because they adjoin state land, both the Loj and JBL afford convenient access to the high peaks (those 4000 ft. or over) and offer a wide choice of trails with a variety of lengths and degrees of difficulty.

ADK's public-service programs are made possible by contributions to the organization and through member support. For further information, write or call the Adirondack Mountain Club, R.R. 3, Box 3055, Lake George, NY 12845-9523; telephone 518-668-4447. ADK Headquarters is located at the southern gateway to the Park off Exit 21 of the Adirondack Northway and offers information about the Forest Preserve as well as the sale of maps and guidebooks.

An hour north of Albany and readily accessible by I-87 (Adirondack Northway) is the Lake George and Southeast section of the Adirondacks. Often bypassed by motorists, it is a region of open rocky summits and ridges offering unencumbered views and many interesting hiking and climbing opportunities. Where can one find a more compelling sight than Lake George surrounded by a quilt of multicolored leaves—reds, yellows, and purples of all descriptions—in autumn?

The Tongue Mountain Range forms a peninsula jutting out into Lake George. Its mountains are, from the north, Brown Mountain, Huckleberry Mountain, Five Mile Mountain, Fifth Peak, French Point Mountain, and First Peak. Across the lake stands Black Mountain, followed by Erebus Mountain, Buck Mountain and numerous smaller peaks.

It must be mentioned that rattlesnakes are occasionally seen on the Tongue Mountain Range and Black Mountain. The timber rattlesnake of New York State is a relatively shy creature, however: It will wish to avoid you even more than you wish to avoid it. They are not likely to be seen along the hiking trails, though normal precautions should be taken. When climbing, take care where you put your hands on ledges. Examine the far side of logs before stepping over them. Be observant in sunny areas, where reptiles are likely to be found. Autumn hikers will find that these cold-blooded reptiles are usually far underground by the time the leaves have turned color.

The other mountains in this section stand out by themselves. Hadley Mountain is farthest south. It is a good mountain to climb in the spring, since its rocky trail has little of the mud so common at that time of year. Pharaoh Mountain, to the north, is reached by one of the many trails that abound in the region around Paradox Lake. Crane Mountain, to the west of Warrensburg, is a delightful climb.

The Tongue Mountain Range

The Tongue Mountain Range Trail has been broken up into three separate day trips. Experienced hikers may wish to combine them for longer outings. For instance, if two cars are available, you may wish to leave one at each end of the trail and hike through to Clay Meadows from the north end. The loop from Clay Meadows to Montcalm Point via French Pt. Mountain and back to Clay Meadows from Northwest Bay is a long 12.8 mi. (20.7 km). It should not be attempted by novices. There is no easy way out should an emergency occur. For experienced hikers, however, this is a tremendously rewarding circuit.

Access to the Tongue Mountain Range is via Rt. 9N. This route may be reached from Lake George Village or by exiting I-87 at Exit 24 and driving east to Rt. 9N. From the junction of the two roads, it is 4.7 mi.

(7.5 km) farther north on Rt. 9N to Clay Meadows. This is 0.2 mi. (0.3 km) beyond the boat-launching site at Northwest Bay. The trailhead at the north end of the Tongue Mountain Range is another 7.3 mi. (11.8 km) north of Clay Meadows, just before the descent off Tongue Mountain begins. DEC signs mark each trailhead. There is parking available at each location.

1. Five Mile Mountain

Round-trip Time—4 hrs. 30 min.
Round-trip Distance—7.0 mi. (11.3 km)
Elevation Change—1258 ft. (385 m)
Summit Elevation—2258 ft. (691 m)
Difficulty—Easy for experienced hikers, moderate for novices.
Map—Bolton Landing (15' quadrangle)

This is a good trip for beginners. Open views reward the climber for much of the way. The tired hiker can turn back at any point and still feel satisfied. There is no water on this route.

Follow blue DEC markers from the trailhead at Clay Meadows. A short distance from the start, the trail makes a sharp left turn off the fire road. There is a DEC register at this location. Continuing, the gently rising trail meets a yellow DEC-marked trail at a junction at 0.65 mi. (1.0 km). The yellow trail leads straight ahead 1.0 mi. (1.6 km). to a lookout at Deer Leap.

Following the blue markers, the main trail bears right, up a slight rise. Several lookouts appear as elevation is gained. Black Ledges is reached at 1.2 mi. (1.0 km). The rocks to the left front offer excellent viewing. Mother Bunch Islands are seen in the lake below and Black Mountain rises to the east. After leaving Black Ledges, you shortly arrive at the summit of Brown Mountain.

A careful observer may be able to see Northwest Bay through the trees to the right. Following open ledges and woods, you reach Tongue Mountain lean-to at 2.6 mi. (4.2 km). It makes a nice resting place. The lichen and flowers found growing on the open rock slopes around the lean-to are fascinating to study or to photograph. Walk on the bare rock as much as possible to protect this vegetation. From the lean-to, marvelous vistas of the Adirondack High Peaks spread out before you to the northwest.

The trail follows rock cairns and blue painted arrows over rock to the right rear of the lean-to. Easy grades lead another 0.7 mi. (1.1 km) over Huckleberry Mountain to a sign in an open spot. Only the remains of a fireplace indicate there was once another lean-to at this location.

The top of Five Mile Mountain is gained at 3.5 mi. (5.7 km). It offers good views of Black Mountain and, beyond it to the northeast, the Green Mountains of Vermont. Outstanding views can be found on the downslopes of the mountain farther to the south.

If a second car has been left at Clay Meadows, it is possible to continue to the four-way junction in the col 1.65 mi. (2.7 km) farther along the trail. It is another 1.95 mi. (3.2 km) to Clay Meadows. This would make a loop totaling 7.1 mi. (11.5 km). There is an 800-ft. (245 m) drop in elevation on a steep trail from Brown Mountain to the junction.

The trail from the north end of Tongue Mountain to the summit of Brown Mountain is also an excellent snowshoeing route. **ADK**

Grasses, Tongue Mountain

Lily, Tongue Mountain

White pine needles, Tongue Mountain

Lichen, Tongue Mountain

2. Fifth Peak

Round-trip Time—3 hrs. 30 min.
Round-trip Distance—5.4 mi. (8.6 km)
Elevation Change—1350 ft. (413 m)
Summit Elevation—1770 ft. (541 m)
Difficulty—Generally easy but steady climbing.
Map—Bolton Landing (15' quadrangle)

Parking is found on the east side of Rt. 9N, just north of Clay Meadows. From the trailhead follow blue DEC markers on a level, and then gradually descending, trail.

You pass through a stand of white pine where interesting ground cover can be seen. A trail junction is reached at 0.4 mi. (0.6 km). Continue straight ahead, now following red trail markers. The tote road now begins to rise at a moderately steep grade through a mixed-wood forest. A cascading brook is crossed on an old bridge.

After five minutes the trail becomes more rocky. Watch for where the trail makes a sharp left and then a sharp right turn. The path then levels. For a while it becomes a pleasant stroll. Gradual climbing begins again at two switchbacks. Downed branches may obscure trail markers in this short section; keep a sharp eye out. A spring is passed on the left as the trail swings upward to the right.

At 1.95 mi. (3.2 km) is a four-way junction. The red trail continues straight ahead, where it eventually descends to Five Mile Point on Lake George far below. The trail left goes 1.7 mi. (2.7 km) up to the summit of Five Mile Mountain.

Follow the blue trail, right, for Fifth Peak. Another 0.55 mi. (0.9 km) farther on, a small sign at a trail junction indicates a side trail to the left. Fifth Peak is 1500 ft. (459 m) along this side trail. A curving path leads you to a lean-to and the marvelous vantage point beyond.

What a magnificent view awaits you: Green islands, like emeralds, glitter below in the deep blue lake. From the grassy lookout, Black, Erebus, and Elephant mountains stand out across the lake. To the south, French Pt. Mountain is prominent.

The Mohawks called the beautiful body of water you are looking at *Andia-to-roc-tee* (place where the lake contracts). Father Isaac Jogues, returning in 1646, christened it Lac Du St. Sacrament (Lake of the Blessed Sacrament). General William Johnson gave the lake its present name, Lake George, in commemoration of King George II.

The delicate appearance of this region reminds one more of the Catskills than the high peaks of the Adirondacks. Hemlocks and white pines are found instead of the expected red spruce and balsam fir. Ground cover and open grassy slopes grace the ridges. The windswept upper reaches provide continuously changing scenes as you hike along. **ADK**

3. Northwest Bay to Montcalm Point

Round-trip Time—4 hrs. 30 min.
Round-trip Distance—10.8 mi. (17.5 km)
Elevation Change—190 ft. (58 m)
**Difficulty—Easy; a long gradual upgrade is found near the end of
   the return trip.**
Map—Bolton Landing (15' quadrangle)

This is a beautiful ramble along an old tote road to Montcalm Point. Fully two-thirds of the trip is along the shoreline of Northwest Bay.

Starting at Clay Meadows, the trail leads off to the east, following blue markers. Gradually descending, it crosses a swampy stream on a long corduroy bridge.

Keep alert for the abrupt turn to the right that the trail takes at 0.4 mi. (0.6 km). A red trail continues straight ahead; your trail swings to the right down a bank. The steady drop in elevation seems nice, but it may appear to be much longer on the return trip.

The variety of plant and animal life makes this an interesting walk. A stream and a marsh are passed. On higher, drier ground the trail parallels the inlet to Northwest Bay for some time. Birdlife abounds here and large waterbirds are commonly seen.

Lacy hemlocks cloak the shoreline. Old axe blazes mark the original route. The path follows the water's edge, occasionally climbing to avoid obstacles but soon returning to the crystalline water. A few streams and one very attractive little waterfall beckon you along the way.

At 5.0 mi. (8.1 km), a trail jct. is reached. The blue trail markers lead left and begin the climb up the ridge, which meanders on for 5.3 mi. (8.6 km) to Fifth Peak lean-to and beyond. Proceed straight ahead to the point.

Montcalm Point is named after the Marquis de Montcalm. His large military force laid siege to Ft. William Henry during the French and Indian Wars. James Fennimore Cooper's *Last of the Mohicans* made this event forever famous. Montcalm was never able to adequately explain why his forces permitted their Indian allies to massacre hundreds of surrendering men, women, and children on that grizzly morning in August of 1757.

From the point, the Narrows of Lake George are seen to the north. Across the lake is Shelving Rock. Erebus Mountain is seen to the north, on the east side of the lake. Buck Mountain rises to the right of Shelving Rock.   **ADK**

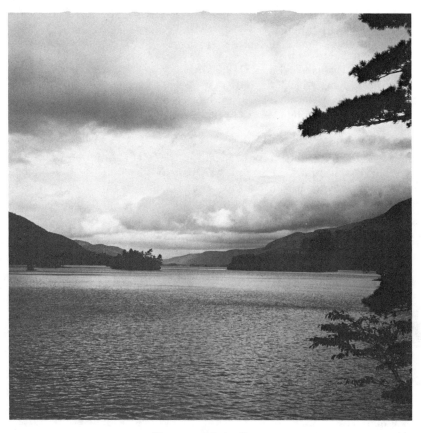

Narrows of Lake George

4. Buck Mountain

Round-trip Time—4 hrs.
Round-trip Distance—6.6 mi. (10.7 km)
Elevation Change—1985 ft. (607 m)
Difficulty—Easy for most part, moderately difficult in a few places.
Map—Bolton Landing (15' quadrangle)

Buck Mountain offers splendid views of the Lake George mountains and the Adirondack peaks far beyond to the north. Unique, however, is the sight sometimes seen from this bald peak when the hiker gazes down at the water below. Dozens of small sailing craft on a sunny summer weekend form ever-changing patterns as sailors exhibit their skills. The spectacle is not soon forgotten.

Access to the trailhead is best gained from the Adirondack Northway (I-87) at Exit 20. Follow Rt. 9 northward a short distance and turn right onto Rt. 149. This is the road to Whitehall. Just past a golf course on the left, turn left onto Rt. 9L. Follow this northward until you come to the right-hand turn for Pilot Knob and Kattskill Bay. This is Pilot Knob Road. Follow it approximately 3.0 mi. (4.9 km) until you see the large DEC sign and parking area on the right for Buck Mountain.

The trail leaves the rear of the parking area. It follows a wide woods road. Passing occasional side trails, it crosses a creek about ten minutes along the way. Alternating grades and leveling-off spots provide quite easy walking. The mixed-wood forests are very pleasant. The smell of hemlock awakens your senses.

A second stream is crossed and at 1.2 mi. (1.9 km) a junction is reached. The trail right leads 3.1 mi. (5.0 km) to Inman Pond and 2.1 mi. (3.4 km) to the Lower Hogtown parking area.

The Buck Mountain trail curves upward to the left and soon reaches a metal pipe on the right, where cool water gushes forth. The route gradually changes from a woods road to a path. Avoid the side trail to the right that soon appears. Yellow DEC markers soon become evident and should be followed.

The first substantial steep grade is soon surmounted, and gradual grades are again the norm. The trail curves left as a wet area is passed. A second and much longer steep grade brings you to the first lookout, on the right from which Crossett Pond is seen to the east.

The walking is now level for about ten minutes. As the grade steepens moderately, you break out on the open rock; views to the east and south begin to appear. Following yellow painted markers ever upward, new sights quickly appear.

The delicate vegetation of the open rock is easily destroyed. Walk on bare rock where possible and don't stray from the trail. Protect this fragile biota.

Still moving upward, the trail drops into a small rock depression and a trail junction is reached. The trail to the right leads on another 2.5 mi.

(4.1 km) to Shelving Rock. Continuing to the left front, the Buck Mountain route leads generally northwest over bare rock to a magnificent outlook just past the high point of rock.

Sailboats flitter about below like water bugs. Crane Mountain is to the west. Prospect Mountain can be seen to the southeast. Across the lake to the north is the Tongue Mountain Range and Northwest Bay. Beyond them stretches the panorama of Adirondack high peaks. Up the lake on the east shore are Erebus Mountain and Black Mountain with its tower just visible. Directly below is Pilot Knob.

As you look downward to the northwest over Little Buck Mountain toward Shelving Rock, it is easy to see why this whole open rock expanse was once called "the deer pasture." **ADK**

5. Black Mountain Loop

Round-trip Time—4 hrs.
Round-trip Distance-6.7 mi. (10.7 km)
Elevation Change—1200 ft. (367 m)
Summit Elevation—2646 ft. (809 m)
Difficulty—Easy climbing, with occasional steepness.
Map—Bolton Landing (15' quadrangle)

"A sentinel, it seems, overlooking the whole lake and mountains round about, the first to welcome the rising sun, and at evening, glowing in the splendor of the dying day, while the valleys below are misty with the shadows of the coming night." This is how Seneca Ray Stoddard described Black Mountain in 1890 in *Lake George and Lake Champlain.* He was right. The highest mountain on the shores of Lake George, it provides an unsurpassed panorama of both the lake and the Adirondacks to the west.

Access to the trailhead is off Rt. 22, north of Whitehall. Approximately 4.5 mi. (7.3 km) north of where Rt. 22 crosses Lake Champlain is a sign for Hulett's Landing. Turn left and proceed 2.7 mi. (4.4 km) to Pike Brook Road. Turn left and travel another 0.8 mi. (1.3 km) along Pike Brook Road. As you begin to descend a hill, the large DEC sign and parking area is seen on the right. This is 3.5 mi. (5.6 km) from Rt. 22.

The trail leads up a slope a short distance to a woods road. Turn left and follow this road 0.5 mi. (0.8 km) to a trail junction just before a private home. From this point the fire tower on top of Black Mountain can be seen. The trail leaves the road to the right and skirts the private property. Do not stray off the trail at this point.

The small red DEC trail markers should be followed. A snowmobile trail with large orange markers winds in and out of the hiking trail. Be sure to follow the smaller trail markers.

The wide woods road you are now following continues gradually upward. A sign soon indicates a side trail left to Lapland Pond. Pass it by and continue straight ahead. Not far beyond this junction the trail forks. The snowmobile trail branches up a hill to the right. The hiking trail drops down a slight grade to the left.

Soon the trail again begins to climb gently. A spring is passed on the right. A rushing brook is soon crossed. The woods road terminates and the trail becomes a footpath. Surmounting a rocky slope, it levels somewhat before winding its way up to the fire observer's cabin and fire tower.

The sight from the summit will long be remembered. The Narrows of Lake George are below you. The Tongue Mountain Range stretches out along the opposite shoreline. Mt. Marcy and her court are seen in the far distance. Elephant Mountain is to the north and Erebus Mountain is to the south. The Green Mountains of Vermont are seen to the east, beyond the southern part of Lake Champlain. Note the color difference between Lake George and this section of Lake Champlain.

If you were to return by the same route, the round-trip distance would be 5.0 mi. (8.1 km). The loop trail provides a much more interesting journey, however.

The trail drops off the west side of the mountain and leads 1.3 mi. (2.1 km) to Black Mountain Pond. This trail descends rapidly with several switchbacks. Outstanding vantage points offer excellent views of the lake below.

Near the base of the mountain you reach a trail junction. Turn left and follow yellow trailmarkers past Black Mountain Pond and then Round Pond. There is a lean-to at the first pond.

As you leave this area, the snowmobile trail is seen again, coming in from the right. Your trail leads straight on, up a small grade. Yellow markers take you onward for another twenty minutes. Keep your eyes on the markers in this section. You will reach Lapland Pond junction. You are now 2.2 mi. (3.6 km) from your starting point.

Turning left from this junction, follow blue markers. The trail soon becomes a woods road again. It is generally level. Eventually you will arrive at a beautiful brook with a bridge over it. Its cooling waters provide a much appreciated respite. A slight grade brings you to the road back to the parking area. Turn right here. It is a little under a mile back to the trail origin. **ADK**

6. Hadley Mountain

Round-trip Time—3 hrs.
Round-trip Distance—4.0 mi. (6.4 km)
Elevation Change—1526 ft. (467 m)
Summit Elevation—2675 ft. (818 m)
Difficulty—Easy, but climbs steadily for the first 1.5 mi. (2.4 km).
Map—Lake Luzerne (15' quadrangle)

Hadley Mountain is a good mountain to take youngsters up since the grade, though steady, is not difficult. The view will certainly make them want to continue hiking. It is also a totally enjoyable mountain to snowshoe on.

Access to the mountain is from the village of Hadley. Hadley is best reached from the east on Rt. 9N. If coming from the west, around the great Sacandaga Lake, follow the Conklingville Road. In Hadley, turn onto Stony Creek Road. Drive north about 3 mi. (4.9 km) until you come to the marked Hadley Hill Road on the left. Proceed along the Hadley Hill Road a little over 4 mi. (6.5 km) until you come to Tower Road. There is a small sign on the right side of the road. This is the second major right-hand turn along Hadley Hill Road. This road descends a long grade for another 1.5 mi. (2.4 km) to the Hadley Mountain trailhead. It is on the left and is marked by a sign. Parking for several cars is available in the summer. In the winter, it will be necessary to squeeze your car to the side of the road so other cars can pass.

The trail follows the fire observer's jeep track up the mountain. The destruction such vehicles cause is readily apparent. The top soil has

Hadley Mountain view in winter

37

been completely stripped away. However, the bare rock makes a relatively dry ascent route even in wet weather. To prevent further erosion, the hiker is urged to stay on the trail and not follow the telephone line.

The red DEC-marked trail starts up through a nice hemlock stand. The steady, easy-to-moderate grade continues for 1.5 mi. (2.4 km) until the top of West Mountain Ridge is reached. The mixed-wood forest trail is interspersed with glacial boulders, small cliffs, and other features. It is an interesting walk.

Once on the ridge top, the trail turns to the right, heading northwest. The last 0.5 mi. (0.8 km) is very open. Superior views make this a pleasant stroll. As the trail curves around the ridge below the fire tower, new vistas continually present themselves to the climber.

The summit is almost entirely open. It is not necessary to climb the tower. The Great Sacandaga Lake is due south. On a clear day the Helderbergs and Catskills can be seen beyond the lake. Some high peaks can be seen to the north from the tower. Pharaoh Mountain and the Green Mountains of Vermont are to the east. Spruce Mountain is to the west. You'll want to spend a long time on the top. Walks along the ridge to the north are quite enjoyable.   **ADK**

7. Crane Mountain

Round-trip Time—4 hrs.
Round-trip Distance—7.4 mi. (12.0 km)
Elevation Change—1154 ft. (353 m)
Summit Elevation—3254 ft. (995 m)
Difficulty—The middle section is quite steep, but most of the rest is easy.
Map—North Creek (15' quadrangle)

This rocky summit provides some stiff climbing but is well worth it. The best way to approach the mountain is by the Wevertown-Johnsburg-Thurman route. From Wevertown on Rt. 28, drive 2.0 mi. (3.2 km) southwest on Rt. 8 to Johnsburg. At Johnsburg turn south onto South Johnsburg Road and proceed 6 mi. (9.6 km) to a T intersection at Thurman. There is a small Crane Mountain sign at this intersection. Turn right onto Garnet Lake Road. Follow this road 1.5 mi. (2.4 km) to where a second, but smaller, Crane Mountain sign indicates another right-hand turn. Travel this good gravel road approximately 2.0 mi. (3.2 km) until it ends at a small parking area at the trailhead. The last half mile (0.8 km) of this road narrows considerably; drive carefully.

The trailhead begins at the road end and a DEC register is seen soon after. There are two trails up the mountain from this point. A short, very steep, trail leads straight ahead from the register. The trail to the left is long but far more interesting. It is this second route that is described here.

From the register, take the fork left along a level track. At 0.4 mi. (0.6 km), this path widens as it merges with an old abandoned woods road. Bearing right, this delightful lane leads after another rolling mile (1.6 km) to a marked intersection near the old Putnam Farm.

Turn right. Soon after this section begins, a natural bridge is crossed. On a hot day the cool breezes emanating from the stream channel's tunnel are very refreshing. Beyond the bridge, one begins a gradual climb that greatly steepens as it approaches Crane Pond.

In the 0.9 mi. (1.5 km) from the Putnam Farm intersection to Crane Pond Outlet, the trail gains some 900 ft. (275 m) in elevation. Views begin to open up and the rocky path requires your attention.

Turn right at Crane Pond Outlet and follow the shoreline. The summit can be seen across the water. At one time the fire observer's cabin was located at this pond's edge. Avoid the cross-over trail to the other summit trail that comes in from the right. Instead, continue around the shoreline to the north. The trail eventually swings away from the pond's perimeter path. After climbing up through the woods, you'll reach a rocky ridge in about 15 minutes. The open ridge trail winds southeast-ward to where the fire tower once stood and offers several outlooks.

Hadley, Blue, Baldhead, and Moose mountains are seen to the south. Indian Lake and Snowy Mountain are off to the northwest. Crane Mountain Pond dominates the view to the west. The return trip might well include a cooling swim in this refreshing body of water.

A shorter, alternate descent to the trailhead is possible by traveling a short distance eastward from the tower. If you can negotiate the nearly vertical drop on a suspended ladder at the onset, you'll find the rest of this route less rigorous. It is, however, challenging enough to keep your attention. **ADK**

8. Pharaoh Mountain

Round-trip Time—4 hrs. 30 min.
Round-trip Distance—9.3 mi. (15.1 km)
Elevation Change—1257 ft. (384 m)
Summit Elevation—2557 ft. (782 m)
Difficulty—Easy for experienced hikers, challenging for novices.
Map—Paradox Lake (15' quadrangle)

From the Adirondack Northway (I-87), take Exit 28. Follow Rt. 74 east a short distance to Rt. 9 and turn right (south). One-half mile (0.8 km) down Rt. 9, turn left onto Alder Meadow Road. This road is about 2.0 mi. (3.2 km) north of Schroon Lake Village.

Keep on this road for 2.2 mi. (3.5 km); at that point, bear left at the fork in the road. Travel another 1.4 mi. (2.2 km) to a parking area at the end. The road is open to the parking area year round. It is a 9.3 mi. (15.1 km) round trip to the summit of Pharaoh Mountain from this point.

Crane Pond Road leads out of the right side of this parking area and runs 1.9 mi. to a parking area near Crane Pond. Currently (1991) it is illegal to drive over this road. A committee has been appointed by the Governor to study this and other roads which penetrate Wilderness-designated areas.

The trailhead is at the end of the parking area, where a register is located. Heading southwest from the register, over a large flat boulder, follow red markers. The outlet of Crane Pond is immediately crossed on a log bridge. The wide trail proceeds over rolling terrain. The mixed woods of hemlock, birch, and beech are particularly beautiful in autumn.

At 0.7 mi. (1.1 km) a trail junction is reached. The Pharaoh Mountain trail makes a sharp right and then a sharp left. Climbing a short rise, you see Glidden Marsh below to the left. This is one of several trout-stocked waters in this region.

A series of gradual rises indicates that you have reached the lower slopes of the mountain. From this point onward, the grades become progressively steeper and longer.

When stopping to rest, look at the rock that makes up this mountain. It is basically a metamorphic gneiss formed from the original granite of the area. Note the alternating bands of light and dark-colored minerals in the rock. There is great variation throughout the mountain, giving clues to what was happening in this area many millions of years ago. The reddish mineral is garnet.

The course of the former telephone line to the tower crosses the trail in several places. Follow the marked trail; it is safer. As you reach the upper third of the mountain, you'll notice the route is mostly over bare rock. When the first good open view, to the west, appears at a rocky shelf to the right, you'll know you are close to the top. One last steep climb, through a grassy area, will bring you to the fire observer's cabin and tower. The tower is currently being used, but how long it will remain open is not known.

The clear, rocky summit is a good place for a leisurely lunch topped off, in season, with the blueberries that appear here. At least three bench markers and one Verplanck Colvin survey marker can be located near the fire tower. Colvin was responsible for the early surveys of the Adirondacks. His enthusiasm and wisdom played a major part in the establishment of the Adirondack State Park. Survey control points on Pharaoh Mountain were used as early as 1878.

Schroon Lake is seen to the west with Spectacle Pond, Desolate Brook, and other smaller bodies of water somewhat closer. A short walk to the southwest brings you to another vantage point from which Pharaoh Lake is seen at the base of the mountain. Treadway Mountain is to the east.

This is an excellent area for snowshoeing and skiing in winter. **ADK**

This section might be called the forgotten part of the Adirondacks. Though few mountains of any great size can be found, good views can be had from those that exist. It is a region of rolling forest, small lakes, and quiet marshes. There is a difference here. You can be alone. In fact, on some trails in this area you might be surprised to meet another person.

This is the land of Nick Stoner and French Louie, legendary woodsmen of yesteryear. Coyotes still abound, and first-time campers have been known to sit bolt upright in their sleeping bags when a loon screamed in the night.

It is good snowshoeing country. Cross-country skiers all have their favorite spots. Hunters come in season, but for the most part the hiker seeking solitude can find it.

The trips described here are easily reached by car. Rts. 8, 10 and 30 provide access into this section.

9. Wakely Mountain

Round-trip Time—4 hrs.
Round-trip Distance—6.0 mi. (9.7 km)
Elevation Change—1635 ft. (500 m)
Summit Elevation—3744 ft. (1145 m)
Difficulty—First two-thirds is easy; the last third is steep and steady.
Maps—Indian Lake and West Canada Lakes (15' quadrangles)
Wakely Mountain (metric quadrangle)

The Wakely Mountain trail is a relatively flat walk on a tote road for two-thirds of its distance. The last third, however, lets you know there is a mountain. In 0.8 mi. (1.3 km) it shoots up 1200 ft. (367 m). The view from the fire tower is outstanding. All points of the compass offer good views.

Access to the mountain is from Indian Lake village. Drive west 2.2 mi. (3.6 km) on Rt. 30. At Cedar River Cemetery, turn left onto Cedar River Road. Proceed on this road for 13.8 mi. (22.4 km). A sign and tote road on the right mark the trailhead at this point. This is not a good road on which to drive, but one can park off it at the trailhead.

Better parking is found if you travel another 0.3 mi. (0.5 km) down Cedar River Road to Cedar River Station. This is the east end of the Moose River Recreation Area at Wakely Dam. It is a good place to park or to camp out. A cool swim, some fishing or canoeing may be added to your hiking agenda here.

The first part of the hiking trail is unexciting. It travels through a sparse woods along a tote road. At 0.7 mi. (1.0 km) the remains of an old

42

T-Lake Falls

logging camp are passed on the left, below the road bank. A road is soon seen to the right and a stream is crossed on a wooden bridge. The route follows the stream for a short distance and then veers away. A junction marked with a Wakely Mountain sign is reached at 1.9 mi. (3.1 km). The trail has gained only about 435 ft. (133 m) elevation at this point.

The fire observer often leaves water jugs here. The water is a most welcome treat, for the remainder of the trail is steep. From this point, very steady climbing begins on the unusually well-cared-for route.

A survey marker is seen on a rock at 2.5 mi. (4.1 km). A short distance farther on you can see the fire tower above you to the right front. Not long after, a side trail to a helicopter pad is passed on the right. Then you arrive at the tower.

The viewing from the ground is restricted to the southeast, but the fire tower provides a 360-degree vista that is very fine. Snowy Mountain is to the southeast. Blue Mountain is to the north. The lake country opens to the west.   **ADK**

10. Snowy Mountain

Round-trip Time—5 hrs.
Round-trip Distance—7.5 mi. (12.2 km)
Elevation Change—2105 ft. (644 m)
Summit Elevation—3899 ft. (1192 m)
Difficulty—Challenging. Long hike, steep much of the way, fatiguing
   if not in good condition.
Maps—Indian Lake (15' quadrangle)
      Indian Lake (metric quadrangle)

Through a joint venture with the DEC and town of Indian Lake, the Adirondack Mountain Club's trail crew greatly improved the condition of the Snowy Mountain Trail in the summer of 1987.

Snowy Mountain just misses being in the 4000-ft. (1233 m) class by a few feet. The vertical climb is actually greater than many of the 46'er peaks, since the base is at a lower elevation.

The mountain is located on the west side of Indian Lake along Rt. 30. It is 6.5 mi. (10.5 km) south of Indian Lake village and 4.7 mi. (7.6 km) north of Lewey Lake Outlet and the boat-launching site. Along the west side of the road, the trailhead for Snowy Mountain climbs a bank. A large paved area is available for parking several cars on the opposite side of the highway.

The trail heads westward up Beaver Brook Valley, following red markers. Generally flat or rolling, it crosses several small streams. Finally, after being within hearing of Beaver Brook down to the right for some time, the path leads below to the rock-bordered stream and crosses it at 1.2 mi. (1.9 km).

A steep climb for a short distance moves you off the valley floor. From this point on, however, the previously closed-in trail opens up and is more pleasant. An extremely large, downed maple blocks the path near the top of the moderating grade. You may have noticed that the largest trees are sugar maples and old spruces. Beaver Brook is again crossed at 1.9 mi. (3.1 km) and young spruces are seen beginning to emerge beneath the branches of the older trees. This is the sign of a climax forest.

Occasional hunting trails branch off, but the main trail is obvious. The route crosses from the right bank of the brook to the left bank. A 2.5 mi. (4.1 km) a tributary is crossed and you begin a long, steady climb up the mountain. The soil thins and is drier. As a result, the trees now become much smaller in diameter.

Gradually the trail becomes rockier. A good lookout to the rear is found at 3.2 mi. (5.2 km). The reconditioned trail is extremely steep for the remainder of the way to the summit. The observer's cabin is reached at 3.8 mi. (6.2 km). A large cliff edge provides a fine view eastward to Indian Lake and beyond. This makes a good place for a lunch break. There is a small spring at wood's edge, near the place where the trail continues to the tower, but its quality varies since the fire observer is no longer here to maintain it.

The summit is only 500 ft. (153 m) up a gentle grade to the south-west. Unfortunately, the tower is no longer open for viewing. A trail southeast of the tower leads to an unusual lookout point where cliffs drop off several hundred feet. Another side trail takes you 50 yds. (46 m) west of the spring to a lookout where Buell and Panther mountains can be seen. The vista down to the ponds along Squaw Brook from this place is exquisite. From the fire observer's cabin, it is possible to see Mount Marcy and the high peaks to the north. **ADK**

11. Echo Cliffs at Panther Mountain

Round-trip Time—1 hr. 30 min.
Round-trip Distance—1.7 mi. (2.7 km)
Elevation Change—725 ft. (212 m)
Summit Elevation—2425 ft. (742 m)
Difficulty—Easy, with some steepness near terminus.
Maps—Piseco Lake (15' quadrangle)
      Piseco Lake (metric quadrangle)

Echo Cliffs at Panther Mountain offer a nice little climb and a surprisingly good view of Piseco Lake and areas to the east.

Access to the trailhead is from the West Shore Road along Piseco Lake. West Shore Road is off Rt. 8, 2.9 mi. (4.7 km) south of where Rt. 8 meets Rt. 10. Drive along West Shore Road 2.6 mi. (4.2 km) from Rt. 8. At this point, a small DEC sign marks the trailhead. There is parking on the opposite side of the road.

The trailhead sign indicates an ascent of 1048 ft. (320 m). This is the vertical distance to the summit, not to Echo Cliffs. Following blue DEC markers, the trail leads through a mature maple-beech forest.

Varying grades provide relatively easy walking for the first 0.6 mi. (1.0 km), until a large boulder is reached. At this point, the way becomes more rocky and consistently steeper. Five minutes later, a large rock outcrop is passed. Soon after, the trail becomes rather steep for the short remaining distance to Echo Cliffs. Red spruce are now present, giving evidence of higher elevation.

View from Echo Cliffs, Piseco Lake

The splendid view is to the southeast. Higgins Bay and Spy Lake are seen to the left front. Beyond Spy Lake, Three Sisters Mountains are seen. To the left is the huge bulk of Hamilton Mountain. A small portion of Oxbow Lake can be seen to the northeast. The long, narrow, curved body of water to the right front beyond Piseco Lake is Big Bay.

Panther Mountain got its name, back in time, when $20 was paid for a "painter" pelt and $10 for a "whelp." There is currently some interest in trying to reestablish this needed predator inside the Adirondack Park. By culling the old and sick, this native cat might strengthen the deer population in this region. **ADK**

12. T-Lake

Round-trip Time—4 hrs. 30 min.
Round-trip Distance—7.3 mi. (11.8 km)
Elevation Change—764 ft. (234 m)
Difficulty—Considerably more rugged than the bare statistics would indicate; a long hike.
Maps—Piseco Lake (15' quadrangle)
Piseco Lake (metric quadrangle)

The hike into T-Lake makes a good day's ramble. It can be lengthened by continuing to T-Lake Falls or by doing a semi-bushwhack trip up T-Lake Mountain. However, for the normal day hike, T-Lake makes a reasonable objective.

Access is from the West Shore Road on Piseco Lake. The trailhead is a short distance south of the entrance to Poplar Point Public Campsite. The trailhead is 4.0 mi. (6.5 km) from the junction of Piseco Road and Rt. 8. This is 1.7 mi. (2.8 km) south of the DEC Northville-Placid signpost in the village of Piseco. Poplar Point Public Campsite makes a good place to leave the car, enjoy a swim after the hike, and perhaps have a picnic supper.

The trail follows red DEC markers up a moderately steep grade. It soon eases somewhat but continues steadily up the shoulders of Piseco and Stacy mountains. At the upper end of this climb two level sections provide respite. Both pass through cols having rocky outcrops. The ferns in the small vlei at the height of land make the second level section especially attractive.

At 1.3 mi. (2.1 km) you begin to descend. The moderate drop soon steepens. Much of your hard-earned elevation is quickly lost. Various branches of Millers Creek are crossed; most are dry. The terrain becomes up and down, and you soon begin the moderate grade up the east shoulder of T-Lake Mountain.

A rocky outcrop on the left draws your attention just before you make an abrupt turn to the left. Now you begin climbing at a moderately steep grade. A few moments later, at 2.6 mi. (4.2 km), the junction with the old trail is reached. It comes in from the right. *Be sure not to take it on your return.*

Bearing left, continue up the curving grade; 0.1 mi. (0.2 km) beyond this point is the branch to the left for T-Lake Mountain. This once popular mountain no longer has a fire tower, so the wooded summit does not offer as fine a view as it once did.

Formerly, the red trail continued up the mountain to the summit while blue markers pointed the way to T-Lake. This change in marker color is the only good way to determine where the old trail up the mountain begins, since no signs are found at this point today. Two small boulders on the left may give enough clue for you to find this trail, which must be considered a semi-bushwhack.

From the junction, follow the blue markers along a nearly level path. You soon catch glimpses of T-Lake, down through the trees to your right. Before you realize it, you are in front of the T-Lake lean-to. The pretty lake is down the bank a short distance.

From here it is another 1.8 mi. (2.9 km) to T-Lake Falls. Reputed to be among the highest waterfalls in the Adirondacks, it is often dry in summer. The trail comes out on the top of the falls. A cable must be used to descend the far side of the waterway to the pool below. At least two people have been killed on these falls, so care is imperative.

Perhaps a respite at the lean-to should be taken before making any decisions about going on to the falls. These trails have been tramped since the 1860s and won't mind waiting a few moments for you to make up your mind. **ADK**

---

13. Wilcox Lake Walk

Round-trip Time—5 hrs. 30 mins.
Round-trip Distance—9.6 mi. (15.6 km)
Elevation Change—480 ft. (147 m)
Difficulty—Easy walking, but a long trip.
Maps—Harrisburg (15' quadrangle)
        Harrisburg (metric quadrangle)

The hike from Brownell's Camp to Wilcox Lake is a woodland ramble at its very best. It follows an old tote road through a magnificent mixed-wood forest. Over half of the trip is along East Stony Creek.

Access to the trail is off Rt. 30, above the Great Sacandaga Lake, on the southern edge of the hamlet of Hope. At 3.2 mi. (5.2 km) north of the Benson Section signpost for the Northville-Placid Trail, turn right on Creek Road. There is a family cemetery plot at this intersection.

Proceed along Creek Road for 2.8 mi. (4.5 km) until a Y-intersection with DEC signs is reached. Turn left onto Mud Creek Road. At its midpoint it will become a dirt road. Proceed along this road 4.9 mi. (7.9 km) to a DEC signpost at the trailhead, along East Stony Creek. Park off the road as much as possible. Do not proceed onto the Brownell Camp property, which is private.

Following blue DEC markers, you will cross Tenant Creek on a good wooden bridge in about ten minutes. The trail is an old logging route through a pretty, mixed-wood forest. After about a mile of walking, you return to the banks of East Stony Creek.

Turning right, the woods road parallels the stream going upstream for close to 3 mi. (9.9 km). In the spring the water is high and fast-moving. Its rocks, sparkling reflections, and ever-changing scenes make it fascinating. In season many flowers are found along the stream banks.

Occasional tributaries are crossed. At one point, the old trail rises far up the bank until it is a considerable distance to the shimmering water below. Some time later you begin the descent to the bridge over Dayton Creek.

Just beyond Dayton Creek, be sure to take the left fork where the tote road splits. Paralleling the stream, you reach the metal suspension bridge that crosses East Stony Creek. It is 4.4 mi. (7.1 km) straight ahead to Harrisburg Lake.

Turning left, cross the suspension bridge and begin the last 0.7 mi. (1.1 km) climb over the low shoulder of Wilcox Mountain to Wilcox Lake. Follow the large yellow snowmobile trail markers carefully in this short section. Switchbacks take you up the steady but moderate slope.

Some blowdown is passed through near the top of the grade, where a T junction is found. The left turn would take you 4.5 mi. (7.3 km) to Willis Lake.

Turn right for the last 0.2 mi. (0.3 km) down the slope to Wilcox Lake. You soon come to the jeep trail, which enters from the right. Continue straight ahead to the DEC register found at the lake's edge.

The lake is good-sized and has good fishing. As you look around this handsome lake, consider that it cost "tenderfeet" $9.00 a week to stay at the Brownell Camp's woods hotel back in 1917. They came by smoky train and dusty stagecoach to spend a season in these climes. You'll probably be home in a nice soft bed tonight, having made the return drive in a few hours. Times were different then, but not necessarily better.

14. Cathead Mountain

Round-trip Time—3 hrs.
Round-trip Distance—2.5 mi. (4.1 km)
Elevation Change—1273 ft. (389 m)
Summit Elevation—2427 ft. (442 m)
Difficulty—A short moderate climb of steady grade, steep near the end.
Maps—Lake Pleasant (15' quadrangle)
       Three Ponds Mountain (metric quadrangle)

Cathead Mountain makes a nice short afternoon's jaunt. Its tower is no longer open. The mountain has been lumbered since at least 1860, when Willard Wright built a lumber mill on its lower slopes. There is yet evidence of the wood cutter but the mountain is an enjoyable climb, generally unaffected by the sawman.

Access to the trailhead is off Rt. 30 in the village of Benson, a few miles above the Great Sacandaga Lake. Turn left towards Benson at the DEC Benson Section sign for the Northville-Placid Trail. Proceed up the long hill 2.8 mi. (4.5 km) to the right-hand turn at North Road. The town hall is at this corner, as is a small DEC sign pointing in the direction of Cathead Mountain. North Road dead-ends at the trailhead 1.2 mi. (1.9 km) farther on. Park on the right so as not to block the private entrance that is on the left.

The red-marked DEC trail follows a dirt road for a short distance and then branches off to the left. A small sign is at this junction.

The gradually rising trail is rather pleasant. About halfway up the mountain the way becomes considerably steeper and very rocky.

A few hundred feet below the summit the fire observer's cabin is reached. From this point one climbs steeply up the bare rock to the fire tower.

It is not necessary to climb the tower in order to gain a good view. To the southeast is the Great Sacandaga Lake. The best views are found in that direction. Groff Mountain dominates to the north. Wallace and Three Ponds mountains are around to the west. All in all, the bare rock of the broad summit provides a most interesting setting for the hiker.

ADK

15. Sawyer Mountain

Round-trip Time—2 hrs.
Round-trip Distance—2.3 mi. (3.7 km)
Elevation Change—650 ft. (199 m)
Summit Elevation—2610 ft. (798 m)
Difficulty—Easy.
Maps—Blue Mountain (15' quadrangle)
      Blue Mountain (metric quadrangle)

Sawyer Mountain is an easy climb. A new trail leads up through a mature forest of maple and beech to the lookout, just past the summit. For such a short climb, the view is very good.

Access to the trailhead is off Rt. 28 between the villages of Indian Lake and Blue Mountain Lake. It is on the west side of the road, 2.6 mi. (4.2 km) north of the bridge across the Cedar River. This is about 6.0 mi. (9.7 km) from Blue Mountain Lake village. The well-marked trailhead has excellent parking facilities.

The trail follows yellow DEC trail markers up rolling grades from the road, leveling off after a few minutes. A moderately steep grade then takes you over a small shoulder of a ridge and down again. Red paint blazes are mixed with occasional trail markers for the rest of the route. Climbing becomes generally moderate for the next half hour.

The pleasant trail passes to the left of a large boulder at 0.9 mi. (1.5 km). The path then levels for a short while and leads to a lookout to the east. The bare rock slope is rather steep and is biased down to the left. Immediately after starting out on the rock, the trail cuts to the right, reentering the woods. Walking is much safer there. The trail farther upslope returns to the open, where good views are found.

Trees become more widely spaced as you approach the wooded summit. The trail goes on another 270 ft. (83 m) past the summit to an excellent lookout.

Below to your left front is Sprague Pond. Beyond it, Blue Ridge extends for several miles. In the valley to your right is a beautiful vlei. Looking due west, between the vlei and the pond, thin Stephens Pond is seen high up on the ridge. The Northville-Placid Trail skirts this pond as it winds 132 mi. (214 km) through the Adirondacks. In the far distance, Blue Mountain boldly stands out on the horizon. **ADK**

EAGLE BAY & BLUE MOUNTAIN SECTION

The Eagle Bay and Blue Mountain section is in the Lake Region of the Adirondacks. The terrain is relatively flat and is more suited to sustaining the wear and tear of the hiker's boots. Though many trails are heavily used, they retain an amazing freshness and primitive quality.

There is something special about this region. It takes hold of you and won't let go. Alvah Dunning, the hermit, lived in the Blue Mountain Lake area in the middle 1800s. Encroaching summer vacationers forced him on to Raquette Lake and, later, to Eighth Lake. When guideboats became too frequent there, he really became upset. He lit out for the Rocky Mountains for peace and quiet. He was back within a year. These lakes had cast their spell over him and he could not stay away.

The lake country mountains are generally not big. You can take your time climbing them and really observe your surroundings. Yet, since the whole region is so flat, excellent views are gained from the summits of these peaks. Rts. 28 and 30 lead into this region.

16. Rondaxe (Bald) Mountain

Round-trip Time—1 hr. 30 min.
Round-trip Distance—2.0 mi. (3.2 km)
Elevation Change—400 ft. (122 m)
Summit Elevation—2350 ft. (719 m)
Difficulty—Easy, with only one minor steep spot.
Maps—Old Forge (15' quadrangle)
Old Forge (metric quadrangle)

The hardest thing about this mountain is figuring out what to call it. At first, it was Pond Mountain. For awhile it became Foster's Observatory in honor of Nat Foster, the trapper. He said he liked to go there to get away from the Indians. After the Civil War, there was a movement by some summer residents to call it Mont. St. Louis. Now, almost everyone calls it Bald Mountain, except for the state officials. To avoid confusing it with another fire tower mountain having the same name, the Conservation Department opted to call it Rondaxe Mountain. Why Rondaxe? Named after a nearby lake, it is the phonetic corruption of the last two syllables of Adirondacks.

On any account, it's probably the most often climbed mountain inside the Park. For sheer fun and ease of climbing, it can't be beat. The summit view is superb.

Access to the trailhead is on Rondaxe Road, off Rt. 28 between Eagle Bay and Old Forge. If coming from Old Forge, Rondaxe Road is a short distance beyond the Bald Mountain Restaurant, where another trail up the mountain begins. Turning west on Rondaxe Road, drive 0.2 mi. (0.3

km) to where there is a large parking area on the left side of the road.

A large, wooden map of the area and a DEC register mark the trail-head. Follow red markers. The first five minutes of walking take you through a hardwood forest on an essentially level trail.

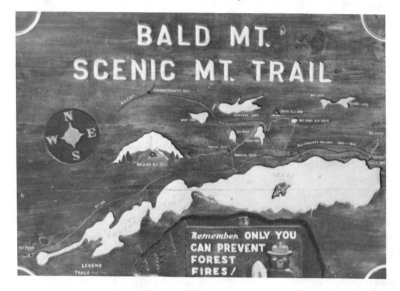

The only steep climbing begins at this point, leading up bare rocks and over tree roots. This short stretch soon moderates. The first lookout is at 0.3 mi. (0.5 km).

Beyond here the climb continuously provides ever-widening views of the Fulton Chain to the east. The ease of climbing combined with frequent looks at the scenery bring you to the summit before you expect it.

The trail follows a hogback ridge. Its spine tapers until, at the last, you feel you are walking up the vertebrae of some great extinct dinosaur.

The rain shelter and fire tower are seen after about 30 minutes of hiking. Below you to the east, large Fourth Lake meets your gaze. As your eyes swing to the right, Fourth Lake constricts to a narrow channel and becomes Third Lake. Second and First lakes are seen farther to the right. Beyond First Lake is Little Moose Lake. Turning back to the far end of Fourth Lake to the left, Blue Mountain looms above the distant horizon 28 miles away. Over 56 miles distant, Mt. Marcy can be seen on a clear day in line with the extreme left margin of Fourth Lake. Algonquin is to the left.

Closer in, Black Bear Mountain is seen just past the end of Fourth Lake. Seventh Lake is to its right . Wakely Mountain may be seen in the distance, over the broad part of Fourth Lake. **ADK**

17. Cork Mountain

Round-trip Time—2 hrs. 30 min.
Round-trip Distance—3.2 mi. (5.2 km)
Elevation Change—470 ft. (144 m)
Summit Elevation—2285 ft. (699 m)
Difficulty—Easy to Carry Pond; moderately strenuous to summit.
Maps—Old Forge and Big Moose (15' quadrangles)
       Old Forge and Big Moose (metric quadrangles)

The Cork Mountain trail is hiked not so much for the view from the summit but for the trail itself. The route is much more a primitive woods path than a broad tote road. It has a certain primeval quality. The closeness of the tree growth, the suddenness with which ponds are reached, and the variation in terrain all combine to make a most interesting trip.

Access to the trailhead is from the same parking area that is used for the Rondaxe Mountain climb. The two trips can be combined easily in one outing. About halfway between Eagle Bay and Old Forge, turn west onto Rondaxe Road. A DEC signpost at this turn indicates the direction of the parking area. Two-tenths of a mile (0.3 km) down Rondaxe Road, the parking area is on the left side of the road. The Cork Mountain trailhead is on the opposite side of the road.

Five minutes after beginning to follow blue DEC trailmarkers, you descend a grade to a junction. Fly Pond is down to the left, visible through the trees. It is worth the brief side excursion to visit it.

The main trail bears right from the junction. It rather significantly winds through the woods, seeming to seek out rock outcrops that can be tramped over. Again you find yourself descending, this time to the edge of Carry Pond. This body of water is much larger than Fly Pond. Turning left, you skirt the shoreline for about ten minutes. In the past there has been a large beaver house at the end of the pond.

Very soon thereafter you come to the old Raquette Lake Railroad bed, at 0.7 mi. (1.1 km). A large wooden placard tells you about this railroad, which was built in 1899.

Having walked for about 30 minutes, you turn right and travel a short distance past the end of Carry Pond to a sign pointing left to Mountain Pond. Following this path, a minor wet area is passed just before you start the ascent.

For the next half hour, the trail progressively steepens. Numerous switchbacks take you up to a junction in a col. Here the blue trail leaves you, dropping down the far side of the ridge to Mountain Pond. You should follow red DEC markers straight up the mountain. In ten minutes, this very steep path brings you to the summit. Two signs point the way to lookouts.

To the northeast, the unusually green Mountain Pond is seen below. A small part of Lake Rondaxe is to the north. In the west is Bottle Mountain.

An interesting extension of this trip can be made if a second vehicle is available at the end of the trail. Dropping down to Mountain Pond, the blue trail continues along an open ridge another 2.8 mi. (4.5 km). There it joins the Bub and Sis Ponds Trail. Going to the right, a 20-minute walk would bring you out on Rt. 28 near Becker's Resort Hotel. **ADK**

18. Windfall Pond Walk and Loop Option

Round-trip Time—1 hr. and 30 min.
Round-trip Distance—2.2 mi. (3.6 km)
Elevation Change—180 ft. (55 m)
Difficulty—Easy.
Maps—Big Moose (15' quadrangle)
Maps—Eagle Bay (metric quadrangle)

The Windfall Pond Trail makes a nice little afternoon hike. It can be extended to a full day's outing if desired. The trail basically parallels the pond's outlet creek. Sometimes high above, sometimes right alongside, it is a pretty path that takes you along the brookside up to the pond.

Access to the trailhead is the large DEC parking area on the Big Moose Road from Eagle Bay. This parking area is on the northeast side of the road 3.3 mi. (5.3 km) from Eagle Bay and 0.6 mi. (1.0 km) south of

Higsby Road.

Starting at the DEC register, follow yellow trail markers along an open level path. After a few moments, you cross a creek on a wooden bridge. As you enter the woods, the narrow trail returns to the stream at 0.7 mi. (1.1 km) and follows the brook much of the rest of the way to Windfall Pond.

It soon climbs a grade far above the water, only to return to it a short time later. To the right of the bridge crossing the stream is an interesting rock cleft through which water cascades in times of runoff.

Turning left across the bridge, the trail parallels the stream. The flow widens to form a vlei in places. At 0.9 mi. (1.5 km) the outlets of Queer Lake and Windfall Pond meet at a swampy area called Beaver Meadow. Here, signs point to the right for both Queer Lake and Windfall Pond.

Following the brook upward another few minutes brings you to Windfall Pond. This pretty little body of water is inundated with white lilies. The purple spikes of pickerel weed brighten the shorelines. Driftwood has collected at the fetch end of the pond.

A full day's outing can be had by going on from the trail junction at Windfall Pond. Following the yellow trail to the left for another 1.6 mi. (2.6 km) will bring you to Queer Lake after joining the red Cascade Pond trail near the lake. After seeing Queer Lake, backtrack on the red trail and follow it past Chain Ponds toward Cascade Lake for 1.4 mi. (2.3 km) to where it meets the blue trail back to Windfall Pond. Turning right, it is another 1.2 mi. (1.9 km) along the blue trail back to Windfall Pond. This would make a total day's walk from the trailhead and return of about 6.5 mi. (10.5 km). **ADK**

---

19. Black Bear Mountain

Round-trip Time—3 hrs.
Round-trip Distance—4.4 mi. (7.2 km)
Elevation Change—542 ft. (181 m)
Summit Elevation—2448 ft. (749 m)
Difficulty—Easy, with one steep section.
Maps—Big Moose (15' quadrangle)
Eagle Bay (metric quadrangle)

Black Bear Mountain is an attractive peak. The first part of the trail runs over the old Uncas Road, built by J. Pierpont Morgan. He and the other elite rode over it to his camp on Mohegan Lake in a coach drawn by six plumed horses. The mountain burned over once, leaving it barren on top. Slowly recovering, much of its summit is a fascinating collection of lichen, blueberries, and mountain ash. Views in all directions are excellent.

Access to the trailhead is on Browns Tract Pond Road, off Rt. 28 in Eagle Bay. Turn north from Rt. 28 at the DEC sign for Browns Tract Ponds Public Campsite. This road bears left almost immediately and becomes

To Eighth Lake Public Campsite

ski trail

BLACK BEAR MT TRAIL

Black Bear Mt

Uncas Rd

ski trail

Browns Tract Pond Rd

Rte 28

a hard-packed dirt road. The trailhead is 2.9 mi. (4.7 km) down this road on the right side. Here, a sign indicates it is 3.5 mi. (5.7 km) to Eighth Lake Public Campsite. There is parking for several cars.

The trail initially follows the Uncas Road, which is now a grassy lane. A short way along this route a cable stretches across the trail. Long, very moderate, grades make progress easy. As you near the bottom of one of these grades, at 0.8 mi. (1.3 km), you see a sign on a birch tree. It points to a side trail at the right. The summit is 1.4 mi. (2.3 km) in that direction.

Turning right, you drop down a moderately steep grade. The otherwise excellent trail has grown in some at this point but soon widens again. Crossing a brook at the bottom of the grade, you proceed along an easy trail. You again drop down a grade and cross another creek at 1.2 mi. (2.0 km).

As you climb a short, moderately steep grade, a ski trail sign is passed on the left. Avoid this turn. Continue straight ahead where you will follow yellow nordic ski trail markers for the rest of the way.

Avoid an unmarked trail to the right a few minutes later, just before reaching a marked junction. The trail to the summit follows the expert ski trail straight ahead. The regular nordic ski trail branches right, running for another 3.0 mi. (4.9 km) to Rt. 28.

The next section of trail is much steeper than anything else to this point. As it winds upward through the trees, there is a branch off left to a lookout. You can walk the rim of the mountain for a short distance before returning to the main trail. Beyond the lookout, the path moderates. It breaks the tree line, covering the last 0.2 mi. (0.3 km) on open rock. Rock cairns guide you where the yellow markers aren't posted. In this section be sure you see the next cairn or marker before leaving the one you've just passed.

The summit is spectacular both for its unusual lichen vegetation and its view. The main vista is to the southeast. Seventh Lake stands out, with large Goff Island at its center. Beyond, Fawn Lake Mountain is seen, with Limekiln Lake to its right. Behind you to the north, Cascade Ridge extends toward Raquette Lake. Blue painted arrows take you a short distance westward over the rocks to another good vantage point. From there, Fourth Lake can be seen. Plan on spending a long time on this most interesting summit.

The trail, and especially the summit section, would appear much more suited for snowshoeing than for skiing. In fact, the trip in over the ski trail from Rt. 28 to the summit would make a nice 6 mi. (9.7 km) round trip. This ski trail begins on Rt. 28 0.9 mi. (1.5 km) east of Brown's Tract Pond Road and is marked by a small sign. The route along Uncas Road is a snowmobile trail in the winter and probably isn't plowed from Rt. 28. **ADK**

---

20. Blue Mountain

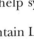

Round-trip Time—3 hrs.
Round-trip Distance—4.1 mi. (6.6 km)
Elevation Change—1579 ft. (483 m)
Summit Elevation—3759 ft. (1150 m)
Difficulty—Moderately difficult; middle section is steep.
Maps—Blue Mountain (15' quadrangle)
    Blue Mountain Lake (metric quadrangle)

Called *To-war-loon-da* by the Indians, this mountain is truly a "Hill of Storms." Its great bulk stands above the surrounding territory like a giant sentinel. In the days of Verplanck Colvin, gunpowder was set off at this summit each evening precisely at nine o'clock to help synchronize the work of his survey crews.

Trailhead access is located on the edge of Blue Mountain Lake village just north of the Adirondack Museum. From the junction of Rts. 28 and 30, this is 1.3 mi. (2.1 km) up the hill along Rt. 30. You'll find a large parking area on the east side of the road.

Trails for Tirrell Pond and Blue Mountain both begin here. Take the red-marked trail to the right along a nearly level woods road. There is a slight increase in grade just before the route becomes a footpath and enters the woods.

Easy grades alternate with level terrain to provide pleasant walking for the next 15 minutes. You then reach a stream crossing. More challenging climbing is found beyond this point.

The way becomes increasingly rocky until you are climbing over solid sheets of bare rock through the forest. It is unusual and comfortable on the feet. The trail becomes very steep for awhile.

The change is most welcome when the trail levels again at 1.5 mi. (2.4 km). Still on bare rock, the path takes you through a pretty coniferous forest for the last 0.6 mi. (1.0 km) to the summit.

While good views are possible from the ground, the fire tower provides magnificent sightings. To the west Blue Mountain Lake is at the foot of the mountain. To its left are Eagle Lake and then Utowana Lake. Beyond the ridges Raquette Lake can be seen. To the north Minnow Pond, Mud Pond, South Pond, and finally part of Long Lake can be traced. In a northeastward direction, Tirrell Mountain, with its beautiful sandy Tirrell Pond, is below you. Just to the left and beyond is Tongue Mountain. Algonquin is in line with Tongue Mountain, another 25 mi. (40.5 km) in the distance. To the right of Algonquin the gap of Avalanche Pass and then Mt. Colden can be seen. Somewhat farther to the left is Ampersand Mountain, seen between Seward and the much closer Kempshall Mountain on Long Lake. **ADK**

21. Cascade Pond

Round-trip Time—3 hrs.
Round-trip Distance—5.6 mi. (9.1 km)
Elevation Change—361 ft. (110 m)
Difficulty—Easy.
Maps—Blue Mountain (15' quadrangle)
    Blue Mountain Lake (metric quadrangle)

Enchanting is the term to describe this trail. It is not the place for hurrying. If you would relax in the midst of beauty, this is the place to do it.

Access to the trailhead is off Rt. 30 east of Blue Mountain Lake village. At 0.9 mi. (1.5 km) from the intersection of Rt. 28 and 30, 0.6 mi. (1.0 km) past the St. Lawrence and Hudson Rivers Divide sign, turn right onto Durant Road. If coming from the east, Durant Road is 2.3 mi. (3.7 km) past the Lake Durant Public Campsite sign and just past the lake itself. Travel 0.2 mi. (0.3 km) down Durant Road to the trailhead sign on the left side of the road. It is just before you reach a cemetery. Your vehicle may be left here or can be parked a short distance down the trail road. Please do not block the passageway.

From the paved road, follow red DEC trail markers a short distance to where an arrow on a sign points to an abrupt turn to the right. Crossing a small brook, the path follows a level route before ascending a tiny knoll.

The trees are an unusual mix. Large hemlocks overshadow the small balsam firs that are coming in. Before you realize it, you are dropping down a slope to Rock Pond. This extension of Lake Durant is crossed on a 200-ft. (61 m) wooden bridge. The white lilies, current-drawn grasses, and purple spiked pickerel weed give you reason to pause. Gazing out on this quiet water, you understand the meaning of "forever wild."

Continuing, you soon surmount a short steep section as you top a little ridge. The trees are now maple and beech. A rather steep but brief descent into the next valley brings you to the second joy of this trip.

For the next twenty minutes, you travel 0.5 mi. (0.8 km) up a delicate valley between two high ridges. The trees are of smaller diameter and are farther apart here. It is like being in a huge amphitheater. Again you feel a distinct urge to walk slowly in order to see everything. It is quite beautiful.

Finally, at the end of the valley, you ascend a moderate slope where the trail becomes essentially level for the remaining 0.9 mi. (1.5 km) to Cascade Pond. You come to a DEC sign 0.5 mi. (0.8 km) from Cascade Pond. Just beyond the sign, bear left. Avoid the unmarked trail to the right.

The trees have now changed to mostly spruce. Cascade Pond is seen at the right a few moments before you reach the lean-to, which sits above the pond. This large beautiful body of water has an active beaver colony.

If a second car is available to the party, a loop ending at the Northville-Placid Trail parking area near the Lake Durant Campsite is possible. By continuing along the pond edge on the red DEC trail for another 0.9 mi. (1.5 km) you will reach the Northville-Placid Trail. Turning left here, follow blue markers another 2.7 mi. (4.4 km) to the Lake Durant Campsite. There are excellent swimming facilities there. Blue markers will take you past the swimming area and on to the roadside parking location. This would make a total loop of 6.4 mi. (10.4 km). **ADK**

Rock Pond in Summer

A- Snowmobile Trail via Stony and
   Sherman ponds to Irishtown
B- Rankin Pond
C- Aiden Lair
D- Lindsey Marsh
E- Boreas River Walk to Hewitt Eddy
F- Hewitt Eddy Loop Trail
G- Vanderwhacker Mountain
H- Forest Ranger Office (closed)
I- Theodore Roosevelt Memorial
J- Tahawus and High Peaks

K- Town of Newcomb Picnic Area
L- Lake Harris Public Campsite
M- Hudson River
N- Newcomb Beach and Boat Launch
O- Santanoni Preserve
P- Newcomb Visitor
   Interpretive Center
Q- Archer & Anna Huntington
   Wildlife Station
R- Nature Trail at Wildlife Station
S- Goodnow Mountain

Boreas
River

Aiden
Lair

To
Hudson
River

Route 28 N

Tahawus

Newcomb

62

The region between Minerva and Newcomb provides an amazing combination of interesting recreational opportunities. To a large extent it has been ignored as hikers followed the major highway systems into the high peaks. Even those traveling to Tahawus and the complex of trails branching northward to Lake Colden and Mt. Marcy seem not to have been aware of what they were passing by.

Reference to the accompanying map will indicate several of the possibilities for outdoor activities. Harris Lake Public Campsite makes a good base for those staying in the area for an extended length of time. Backpackers and cross-country skiers will find Santanoni Preserve very satisfying. The Newcomb Visitor Interpretive Center is a wonderful place to spend a day learning about the Adirondacks and wandering beautiful trails.

There are canoe and boat access sites at both Newcomb and Harris Lake. Mountains with spectacular views of the high peaks are found here. Charming jaunts into flowering marshes and along gurgling brooks make delightful day trips. All things considered, this is a splendid place to enjoy nature.

The sequence of trips provided in this section begins where the Olmstedville Road intersects Rt. 28N at Minerva. It continues along Rt. 28N northwestward to Newcomb and slightly beyond.

22. Rankin Pond

Round-trip Time—30 min.
Round-trip Distance—0.8 mi. (1.3 km)
Elevation Change—100 ft. (32 km)
Difficulty—Easy, with some gradual ascent on the return.
Maps—Newcomb (15' quadrangle)
　　　　Newcomb (metric quadrangle)

A small turnoff with a signpost is found at the trailhead on the west side of Rt. 28N, 4.3 mi. (6.9 km) north of Minerva. There is a small parking area on the opposite side of the road.

The blue-marked trail turns abruptly left almost immediately and wends its way through a hardwood forest. It soon begins a gradual descent over a rocky path and quickly reaches the water's edge.

A small shoreline clearing lends a magnificent view of the pond. The distant shore is cloaked with blueberry bushes. Water plants gracefully reach up through the water to the sky above. It's a quiet place and quite beautiful. **ADK**

63

23. Boreas River Walk

Round-trip Time—1 hr. 30 min.
Round-trip Distance—2.2 mi. (3.6 km)
Elevation Change—20 ft. (6 m)
Difficulty—Easy.
Maps—Newcomb (15' quadrangle)
      Newcomb (metric quadrangle)

Many years ago there was a state campsite on the Boreas River where it crosses Rt. 28N. Today only a few remaining fireplaces give witness to the past. The river crossing is 8.7 mi. (13.9 km) from Minerva. Recently a new concrete bridge was built across the river. The approach to the old bridge makes a good parking area. It is adjacent to the old campsite.

The trail begins on the west side of the road, opposite the parking area. It follows red DEC markers along the river bank for the whole distance. The stream's varying sounds are intriguing. First silent, then noisily rushing, it continuously whets your curiosity. Numerous little side trails lead to the river's edge and interesting sights. One notices the fragrance of the conifers and the softness of the earth beneath one's feet.

It's hard to imagine that this little stream once carried thousands of logs downstream each spring as dammed meltwaters were released. Log drivers, mostly French Canadians, leapt nimbly from log to log as they worked to prevent jams.

The trail rambles on with but a single rise above the river. At one point the rushing water draws you to a rocky waterfall. Occasionally a small tributary is crossed.

At the 1.1 mi. (1.8 km) point, the Hewitt Eddy Loop Trail joins the Boreas River Trail at Hewitt Eddy. Do not stray from the river's edge unless you wish to make the loop hike. The Hewitt Eddy Loop Trail runs 0.75 mi. (1.2 km) farther through the woods to Rt. 28N, some 0.6 mi. (1.0 km) south of the Boreas River bridge. If both trails are to be walked, it is suggested that you start at the Hewitt Eddy Loop Trail trailhead.

It was once possible to proceed farther downriver for a different view of Hewitt Eddy, but that section is no longer maintained.

24. Vanderwhacker Mountain

Round-trip Time—5 hrs.
Round-trip Distance—5.8 mi. (9.3 km)
Elevation Change—1650 ft. (495 m)
Summit Elevation—3385 ft. (1016 m)
Difficulty—Moderate for experienced hikers, possibly challenging
  for novices.
Maps—Newcomb (15' quadrangle)
    Newcomb (metric quadrangle)

Named after an early pioneer who lived at the base of the mountain, Vanderwhacker Mountain stands alone. Its summit presents a beautiful vista to the north, where the high peaks rise.

The approach is a gravel road on the west side of Rt. 28N. This is 8.8 mi. (14 km) from Minerva, just across the Boreas River bridge. A small DEC sign and a mailbox mark the turnoff.

This road immediately climbs a steep, loose-gravel slope. Once this hazard is surmounted, the remainder of the 2.6 mi. (4.2 km) drive is better. The driver must, however, use normal caution. Traveling through a beautiful coniferous forest, one feels no desire to rush, anyway. Avoid the left-hand turn at 1.5 mi. (2.4 km) just before crossing Vanderwhacker Brook on a small bridge. There are several open campsites with picnic tables and fireplaces in this area.

The road bears right, crossing a railroad track. One notices the road narrowing and more care is required from this point onward. At 2.6 mi. (4.2 km) a right turn abruptly brings you to a small parking area, a picnic table, and the trailhead. This is the first turnoff since the railroad tracks; it is marked by a very crude sign reading "Vanderwhacker Mountain."

Following red DEC markers, the trail gradually climbs through a hardwood forest. Soon leveling off, it swings right as it skirts a swampy area and crosses two small streams.

More gradual inclines then take you upward for another 20 minutes. Just after crossing a stream at 1.3 mi. (2.1 km), the grade steepens and you can see the fire observer's cabin up the open slope. The snowmobile trail turns left, below the cabin, but the hiking trail passes between the buildings and continues uphill. Situated on a grassy grade, the cabin is a good place to take a rest.

The route leads past the buildings and is much steeper for some distance. Eventually it moderates and finally becomes a path along a narrow ridge. This is a marvelous section of the trail. With the open sky above and the trees sloping off steeply below on each side, it is exhilarating.

Various small herbs and flowers grow here. Occasional ferns add to the scenery. When present, balmy breezes make the setting complete.

Becoming steeper again, the trail ascends one last stretch before emerging at the small sharp peak. It is closed in by trees on three sides, but open views are clear to the north. The fire tower is again open, and the panorama is most rewarding. Algonquin and Avalanche Pass stand out. Mt. Colden, Redfield, Marcy, Haystack, Allen, Gothics, Sawteeth, Nippletop, the Boreas Range, Dix, McComb, and countless minor peaks are evident. Plan on staying on top for awhile.

In winter, the approach road would be an excellent cross-country skiing area through to Moose Pond. It also would be a good climb up the mountain on snowshoes.

Roosevelt Memorial Tablet. A stone monument with a metal tablet honoring President Theodore Roosevelt is located on the north side of Rt. 28N, 12.7 mi. (20.3 km) from Minerva. This is 2.2 mi. (3.5 km) from Newcomb.

On September 6, 1901, President McKinley was wounded in an assassination attempt in Buffalo, New York. Assured that McKinley was recovering, Vice-President Roosevelt struck out for the Tahawus Club and Mt. Marcy. On Friday, September 13th, his climbing party, having ascended Mt. Marcy, was enjoying lunch at Lake Tear of the Clouds when a messenger burst out of the woods and informed Roosevelt that McKinley had taken a turn for the worse.

This resulted in a hasty withdrawal to the Tahawus Club and an eventual midnight race by horse-drawn carriage to a train standing by at North Creek, ready to speed him off. The monument marks the approximate spot Roosevelt had reached in his dash through the night when, at 2:15 a.m. on September 14th, McKinley died and Roosevelt became President.

ADK

Roosevelt Tablet

66

25. Archer and Anna Huntington Wildlife Forest Station Nature Trail

Round-trip Time—1 hr.
Round-trip Distance—0.5 mi. (0.8 km)
Elevation Change—15 ft. (4.6 m)
Difficulty—Very easy.
Maps—Newcomb (15' quadrangle)
       Newcomb (metric quadrangle)

This nature trail is located 2.5 mi. (4 km) west of the Santanoni Preserve signpost in Newcomb on Rt. 28N. It is open for use from approximately June 15th until October 15th each year.

The trail has been developed by the students and staff of the SUNY College of Environmental Science and Forestry of Syracuse University. The station is a research unit of the college. At the beginning of the trail are a parking area and small building where trail guides are kept.

Though only about 0.5 mi. (0.8 km) long, the trail is well designed. Numbered markers along the route correlate with the guidebook to help identify plant life. Beaver dams, spruce flats, and glacial boulders may be seen. Over 170 species of birds have been sighted in this area, and the most commonly observed ones are listed. Leaf drawings simplify the identification of trees.

This is an especially nice place for young children to visit. The distance is short enough to retain their attention and the experience can be most educational. It is an excellent opportunity for parents to teach good forest behavior. Remember the saying, "Take only pictures and leave only footprints." **ADK**

26. Goodnow Mountain

Round-trip Time—2 hrs. 15 min.
Round-trip Distance—3.0 mi. (4.8 km)
Elevation Change—1060 ft. (324 m)
Summit Elevation—2685 ft. (806 m)
Difficulty—Easy for experienced hikers, moderate to easy for novices.
Maps—Newcomb (15' quadrangle)
Newcomb (metric quadrangle)

Perhaps no other mountain in the Adirondacks offers such a rich reward for so little effort. This marvelous little mountain is truly a gem. The trail shows excellent examples of good trail maintenance techniques. About five minutes along the trail the Catskill Forest Association has an interesting exhibit explaining clear-cutting techniques. A small sign on the south side of Rt. 28N, 4 mi. (6.4 km) west of the Santanoni Preserve sign in Newcomb, marks the trailhead. The trail is closed each year from October 15th until the end of big-game hunting season. No motorized equipment is allowed. Hikers are to keep on the trail, since this is private property.

The trail follows red markers over land of the Archer and Anna Huntington Wildlife Forest Station. The gravel road you initially follow bears to the right after only about 150 ft. (45 m), but the summit trail goes straight ahead up a moderate slope. Becoming a moderately steep grade, the climbing is steady for about 15 minutes on a hard-packed track. The welcome leveling-off that follows gives you a breather.

Maple, birch, and other hardwoods make up the larger growth. These trees generally appear in an orderly plant succession after the original wood has been lumbered. The specific tree species and their diameters tell something of how long ago the cutting took place. Notice the occasional red spruce sprouting up here and there. It is a sign that the native trees are gradually reclaiming their land.

The trail swings around a very large boulder on the left. Quite a bit of corduroy (wooden cross ties) is seen. Becoming steeper again, the trail traverses some bare rock. Turning abruptly to the right and widening to a tote road, the trail passes a metal storage shed on the right. An open view can be obtained from a rock outcrop behind this building.

The woods open up as the tote road winds its curving course upward. This section is easily traveled and is rather attractive. Massive rocks form cliffs on the right with beds of fern at their feet. A short path leads to the right, where an old covered well stands. The road now curves back to the left. An arrow on a Goodnow Mountain sign directs you to a narrowing path where a second building is passed.

Your route is now along the side of a ridge and is a pleasant journey. Views begin to open up. In a few moments, you drop down into a small col. Avoid a side trail to the left which follows the col downward. Far below in the distance is Rich Lake. Its deep-blue color is in sharp contrast to the emerald green of the forest trees.

A tower sign points straight ahead, and another five minutes along this trail brings you to the fire tower and the cabin of the observer. The mountain is fairly open on its rocky top. Absolutely spectacular views are available to the west, north, and east. Climbing the fire tower extends your sighting radius to a full 360 degrees.

All of the High Peaks are visible past the beautiful waters of Rich Lake. To the east, Vanderwhacker's fire tower can be spotted. Far to the west, Long Lake flows northward. As Robert Wickam once said while speaking of another area, "After gazing awhile, the inclination comes to murmur amen."

It would seem that a winter trip up Goodnow Mountain would be tremendously interesting. The trail is wide and easily followed. It is a short trip, but Santanoni Preserve is nearby should additional exercise be desired.

Newcomb Visitor Interpretive Center.

This center is a marvelous place for both young and old to learn more about the Adirondacks. Workshops, scheduled lectures, and group classes are available year-round. Audio-visual displays in the main building, computer-assistance systems for selecting desired activities throughout the Adirondacks, and picnic tables outside make for a pleasant day.

Three beautiful trails run along Rich Lake with information posts at regular intervals. Numerous vistas offer seats where the walker can rest, enjoy the scenery, and perhaps think about nature.   **ADK**

High Peaks from Goodnow Mountain

View from Hurricane Mountain

The Keene-Keene Valley section epitomizes the Adirondacks for mountain climbers. It is in this region that many of the "High Peaks," those over 4000 ft. (1223 m), are found. It is here that Orson Schofield ("Old Mountain") Phelps had the feeling of "heaven up-h'istedness" as he gazed from "O'Mercy" (Mt. Marcy).

This results in a curious imbalance, however. While the masses are climbing the giants, the most casual glance at a map will indicate dozens of other peaks that are nearly neglected. If these "little giants" were in other parts of the Adirondacks, they would be scaled far more frequently. It is from these oft-forgotten mountains that many of the truly panoramic views of the Adirondack Range are found. The hikes described here are representative of the variety of outing opportunities in this region.

Access to this section is by Rts. 73 and 9N, off Exit 30 of the Northway (I-87).

27. Sunrise Trail to Gilligan Mt.

Round-trip Time—3 hrs.
Round-trip Distance—2.2 mi. (3.6 km)
Elevation Change—670 ft. (204 m)
Summit Elevation—1420 ft. (433 m)
Difficulty—Short, steep slopes alternating with long, gradual sections.
Maps—Elizabethtown (15' quadrangle)
       Elizabethtown (metric quadrangle)

This mountain is a jewel snuggled in the shadow of much higher peaks. Formerly known as Sunrise Mt., its trail has remarkable variation and vegetation. A series of rock outcrops provide superb views throughout the ascent. It has a few short steep sections, but they are a small percentage of the whole trip.

Trailhead access is from Exit 30 of the Adirondack Northway (I-87). Head northwest on Rt. 73 toward Lake Placid. At 2.4 mi. (3.9 km), bear right at the large jct. Continue northeast on Rt. 9. Pass over a small bridge at Split Rock Falls at 4.7 mi. (7.6 km). This is a good swimming spot to cool off at after the climb. Near a dirt road jct. on the east side of Rt. 9 at 6.0 mi. (9.7 km) is a small, green "Gilligan Mt." sign and a Public Fishing Area parking area. Park here and follow the dirt road across the bridge over the Boquet River. Past the bridge, bear right and continue another 250 ft. (91 m) to the Gilligan Mt. trailhead on the left side of the road.

The trail is a flat path which soon crosses a lumber road. It continues on the level through attractive deciduous forest until a moderately steep section is reached at about 0.1 mi. Varying grades and level zones then alternate, passing large boulders and viewing spots at rock outcrops. Just as one begins to huff and puff, a change of pace or a nice view appears to ease the situation.

The first of several dips in the trail is found at 0.3 mi., with an accompanying short, steep climb out of the low spot. The route changes direction occasionally and there is a sharp dropoff to the left at 0.45 mi. Soon Rt. 9 can be seen in the valley below.

Past lumbering has created open spots where sunlight can reach the forest floor; here seasonal flowers in bright array provide interesting studies for the botanist. A beautiful lichen garden graces a lookout spot at 0.6 mi. A series of dips and lookouts, with occasional rock cairns to guide you, takes you ever higher. Volcano-like Hough and the large bulk of McComb and East Dix are now apparent on the west-southwest skyline. The pathway eases in difficulty until a last steep "up" takes you to a wide open-rock lookout at 1.0 mi.

This is the usual endpoint of the hike, although there is a final trail sign on a tree a short distance ahead. The enthusiastic hiker can continue beyond that point on several herd paths another 0.1 mi. to the actual summit, but trees prevent a view.

All in all, this little mountain, maintained by the Schenectady Chapter of ADK, is a wonderful climb of moderate difficulty and short duration, with widely varying views and botanical interest.   **ADK**

---

28. The Brothers Trail and Loop Option

Round-trip Time—5 hrs.
Round-trip Distance—5.0 mi. (8.1 m)
Elevation Change—2198 ft. (672 m)
Summit Elevation—3721 ft. (1138 m)
Difficulty—Moderately difficult, but steep in one place.
Maps—Mt. Marcy (15' quadrangle)
**   Mt. Marcy (metric quadrangle)**

The following trail description is in two parts. The hiker who wants absolutely beautiful scenery in the context of an afternoon jaunt over bare rock is advised to take the hike up to the summit of the Third Brother. On the other hand, the well-conditioned hiker who wants a full day's trip couldn't choose a nicer way to spend the day than to tramp the loop option.

Access to the trailhead is off Rt. 73. Turn at the large DEC "Trails to the High Peaks" sign in the village of Keene Valley. Drive 1.6 mi. (2.6 km) to the parking area, called the Garden. The Garden is one of three primary points of entry into the High Peaks.

It may be well to point out that at the Garden some of the obvious contrasts between High Peaks hiking and hiking in other areas of the Adirondacks will be felt. You'll immediately realize that many people are using the area. Finding a parking place may be difficult. A park ranger may be on duty here to help and advise hikers. Before starting out, be sure that you have plenty of drinking water.

The trail begins at the right rear corner of the parking area, following red ADK markers up a moderately steep slope. Be careful not to take the yellow Phelps trail, which starts at the left rear of the parking area.

The grade soon levels to a moderate grade and a pleasant walk takes you through the white birches above Juliet Brook. After 20 minutes, the trail turns left and drops down to the stream. Soon after crossing Juliet Brook, the hardest climbing of the trip begins. Becoming a steep grade, the trail swings to the left between two boulders. At rock outlooks, you have excellent views of Hurricane Mountain to the northeast and Giant to the east. Mt. Marcy is in the southeast.

From 1.2 mi. (1.9 km) onward, there is mostly open rock climbing to the flat summit of First Brother. Here, Johns Brook Valley spreads before you. Across the valley the Great Range of Lower and Upper Wolf Jaw, Armstrong, and Gothics are seen.

The trail descends slightly and then continues gradually upward to the summit of Second Brother. A good outlook is found 20 yds. (18 m) off the trail to the right.

The path enters trees and drops through a birch and fern woods. From here it again heads upward toward the summit of the Third Brother. The appearance of balsam fir tells you that higher elevations are being reached. From the Third Brother, which is more closed in than the other summits, the profile of the bare slide of Big Slide Mountain stands out before you. There is no other peak quite like Big Slide in all of these mountains. *The afternoon hiker is advised to go no further.* The return route provides different perspectives of interesting scenery.

The well-conditioned hiker who wishes a longer trip may well continue. The whole loop from The Garden takes approximately seven hours to complete. From this point onward, the trail is harder to navigate and is in poorer condition.

The continuing path drops into a balsam fir and spruce forest. At 2.7 mi. (4.4 km) a natural rock shelter is seen on the left. The col is reached 15 minutes later. A gradual climb to the junction with Slide Brook Trail now begins.

The junction is reached at 3.6 mi. (5.8 km). From here, the hiker may turn right for another optional side trip. It is an extremely steep 0.3 mi. (0.5 km) to the summit of Big Slide Mountain. If you have the energy, it is worth the extra time to make the trip.

Turning left down the Slide Brook Trail, descend the slopes through berry bushes to the floor of Johns Brook Valley. Views of the Great Range are frequently seen through the trees across the valley as you follow Slide Brook. A spring is passed soon after beginning this stretch, but it doesn't always have water. Slide Brook appears halfway down the slope and is crossed and recrossed many times.

When the Phelps Trail is reached, a left turn takes you back toward your starting place at the Garden. You may wish to turn right and take the short 10-minute walk to Johns Brook Lodge (JBL). JBL, a wilderness lodge owned and operated by the Adirondack Mountain Club, is unique to the Adirondacks and well worth seeing.

Yellow markers take you along Johns Brook on your return to the Garden. Soon after crossing Slide Brook for the last time, you will see Howard lean-to on the right. Another few minutes down the trail, a trail junction is reached at the ranger's cabin. Take the branch to the left and continue following yellow markers.

Rolling terrain with occasionally moderate grades will be traversed for the last 3.0 mi. (4.9 km) of this outing. This attractive, though heavily traveled, section passes through hardwood forests.

Three large boulders are reached 1.4 mi. (2.3 km) from the Garden. One is often used for emergency shelter, as the blackened smoke on the overhang indicates. Deer Brook lean-to is soon reached after a short, steep little climb from the brook. Another 15 minutes of walking brings you to Bear Brook lean-to. From here, a persistent decline in elevation eases the way for the last 0.9 mi. (1.5 km) to the Garden.   **ADK**

THE BROTHERS LOOP TRAIL

29. Hopkins Mountain via Mossy Cascade Brook

Round-trip Time—4 hrs. 30 min.
Round-trip Distance—6.3 mi. (10.3 km)
Elevation Change—2120 ft. (648 m)
Summit Elevation—3183 ft. (973 m)
Difficulty—Moderate, perhaps challenging for the novice.
Maps—Mt. Marcy and Elizabethtown (15' quadrangles)
      Keene Valley (metric quadrangle)

The walk to the waterfalls on Mossy Cascade Brook is charming. The climb along the brook is through hemlock; frequent lookouts and seasonal blueberries add to the pleasure, topped off with an open summit from which 22 major peaks are visible up through the Ausable Lakes and Johns Brook valleys.

The trailhead is off Rt. 73, 0.4 mi. (0.6 km) towards Keene Valley from the Ausable Club entrance sign at St. Huberts. Park at the next St. Huberts side road, 0.1 mi. (0.2 km) from the trailhead. A green and white ATIS signpost and trail markers on the north side of Rt. 73, where the bank drops from the road, mark the trail.

The trail crosses Crystal Brook and then follows above the East Branch of the Ausable through woods until it nears a home at the left at 0.4 mi. (0.6 km). Swinging right onto a tote road, it immediately turns left to another old road. Finally, the trail bears right at a junction and curves southeast over flat terrain.

The trail leaves the road at 0.5 mi. (0.8 km) and follows the left bank of Mossy Cascade Brook. (Soon a side path left is reached, leading 200 yds. to the base of Mossy Cascade Brook Falls.) The summit trail bears right, passes to the left of a private camp, and then heads up several steep pitches.

The first open lookout is reached at 1.5 mi. (2.4 km). The route then descends into a col before climbing to another broad ledge where more viewing is possible.

The trail moderates before reaching the Ranney Trail junction at 2.3 mi. (3.7 km). (The Ranney Trail heads left 1.8 mi., 2.9 km, to Keene Valley.) The route enters a ravine between Hopkins and Green mountains. It reaches another junction at 3.0 mi. (4.9 km). Turn left. (The trail right leads 3.0 mi., 4.9 km, to the summit of Giant Mountain.)

The trail climbs very steeply from this junction for a short distance. It then moderates and runs over open rock to the summit. The view up the Ausable Lakes Valley and Johns Brook Valley is magnificent. Enjoy lunch and don't eat all the blueberries.

From the summit, a trail leads northwest 0.7 mi. (1.1 km) to the lookout near the summit of Spread Eagle Mountain and then another 1.7 mi. (2.8 km) to the Beede Road trailhead in Keene Valley. **ADK**

30. Hurricane Mountain

Round-trip Time—4 hrs. 30 min.
Round-trip Distance—5.3 mi. (8.6 km)
Elevation Change—2000 ft. (611 m)
Summit Elevation—3694 ft. (1130 m)
Difficulty—A moderate rate of climb for a fairly long ascent distance.
Maps—Elizabethtown (15' quadrangle)
Elizabethtown (metric quadrangle)

The Indian name for Hurricane Mountain is *No-do-ne-yo*, Hill of Wind. Its vast bulk is often buffeted by strong air currents. Alfred Billings Street, the famous lawyer and librarian of 19th-century Adirondackana, commented on this in his book, *The Indian Pass:* "It put me in mind of the Scripture question, 'What went ye out in the wilderness to see? A reed shaken with the wind?' No, but a crest shaken (nearly) with a whirlwind. Most appropriately named is that peak. The wind fairly poured a torrent over it. I have an indistinct recollection of dim shapes and fluttering garments huddling together for mutual protection from the wolfish blasts, while I clutched the rim of my hat with the clutch of desperation. But the view was superb."

Carry a jacket or sweater with you for comfort at the summit. Pick a good day and enjoy that superb view. It's one of the best in the mountains.

The trailhead is on the north side of Rt. 9N, 3.6 mi. (5.8 km) east from Rt. 73 and 1.6 mi. (2.6 km) past Hurricane Road. This is 6.8 mi. (11.0 km) west from Elizabethtown. It is marked by a small DEC signpost and there is a parking area on the opposite side of the road.

The trail follows red DEC trail markers. It immediately climbs steeply up from the road for about 15 minutes. Leveling off, the way then becomes a footpath. Passing through a pretty coniferous forest, you cross two streams on bridges before reaching a minor wet area. Beyond this two more bridges are crossed.

Having traveled easily a little over a mile (1.8 km), you will now find climbing more challenging. Heading up a ridge, long moderate grades with periodic respites take you upward. Take care to follow markers straight up the mountain when you reach the small blowdown section. Do not extend the false trail to the left, as some earlier hikers have done. Another wet section is crossed on corduroy as you approach the 2.0 mi. (3.2 km) point.

Once past this section, climbing picks up again. The change from coniferous to birch trees at this elevation is a reminder of past forest fires. Just before joining the ADK North Trail from the Mountain House, the trail again steepens sharply and is quite rocky.

Turning right at this junction, the trail levels and the last 265 yds. (243 m) to the summit pass through wind-stunted spruces to the bare rock. Paint blazes now take you generally to the left and guide you to the base of the fire tower. A full-circle panorama makes it unnecessary to climb the tower.

To the north you can see the Jay Range. The Green Mountains of Vermont spread out beyond Lake Champlain in the northeast. Directly southward is Knob Lock, with the ridge of Green Mountain beyond it. Giant and Rocky Peak Ridge are still further off. Dix, Nippletop, the Great Range, and finally Mt. Marcy are seen as your gaze swings southwestward. Mt. Colden and the MacIntyre Range are seen next. These are followed by Cascade and Porter. Pitchoff is due west, with distant Ampersand just to its left. Whiteface Mountain is northwest. Lesser peaks, too numerous to list, are found in all directions. **ADK**

---

31. Balanced Rocks on Pitchoff Mountain

Round-trip time—2 hrs. 30 mins.
Round-trip Distance—3.1 mi. (5.0 km)
Elevation Change—882 ft. (270 m)
Summit Elevation—3022 ft. (924 m)
Difficulty—Half is easy, half is on a very steep eroded trail.
Maps—Mt. Marcy (15' quadrangle)
Mt. Marcy (metric quadrangle)

The Balanced Rocks on Pitchoff Mountain provide both a climb and viewing location that are quite unusual. The hiker should be prepared for some steep climbing and an eroded trail. The small ridge that holds the Balanced Rocks has an appearance more of the Swiss Alps than of the Adirondacks. Expect an interesting outing.

Access to the trailhead is off Rt. 73 at the north end of Upper Cascade Lake. This is 4.5 mi. (7.3 km) east of Heart Lake Road. Park in the area provided at the Cascade Mountain trailhead and climb the Pitchoff Mountain trail directly across the road.

Red DEC trail markers take you up a moderately steep grade for about five minutes. The route then levels for the next 0.5 mi. (0.8 km). You first find an attractive open maple stand and then a spruce-birch wood.

About 20 minutes after starting your climb, you ascend a steep pitch to a small lookout at the right. Cascade Mountain stands out. Another longer pitch brings you to a better lookout, where both Cascade Lakes are clearly seen in their glory below. The sharp cut in Cascade Mountain between the two lakes was the original trail up that peak. It leads to the cascade of water from which the mountain gets its name.

Moving along the ridge side, you soon drop down to a flattened depression, which is quickly crossed. Steep climbing then begins. After ascending one such section, the trail swings left on the level for a short distance. A second steep eroded section follows, until you reach the bare rock face of a near vertical slope at 1.1 mi. (1.8 km).

The old trail to the right is considered dangerous. The safer route fol-

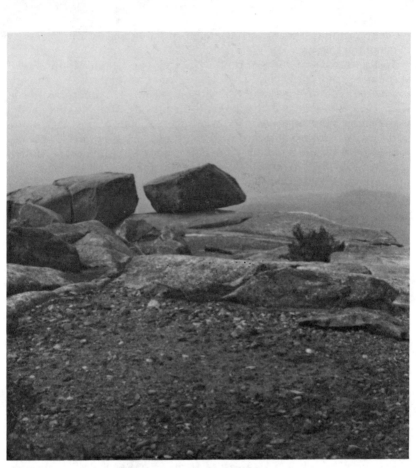

Balanced Rocks, Pitchoff Mountain

lows red markers to the left. Here, you spend the next 15 minutes sidling around the bald wall of the mountain. You soon descend slightly, and then begin a moderate, but steady, climb to the upper end of the rock massif. It is reached at 1.4 mi. (2.3 km).

Turn right for Balanced Rocks. On a welcome level stretch the whole character of your surroundings makes a dramatic metamorphosis. Low conifers thin out as you move toward the end of the ridge. A barren, windswept aura of desolation develops. Void of vegetation, the two great balanced rocks perch at the extreme point of the ridge, seemingly ready to fall into the great abyss below. Giant eroded joint patterns in the rock floor give the whole scene an appearance of being ready to collapse at any moment, but they have been this way for millennia. Beyond Balanced Rocks, the ridge's vast rounded edge juts toward Lake Placid in the distance.

To the left stands Cascade Mountain, overshadowing all else. Algonquin is seen behind her, along with Big Slide, Colden, and Marcy. Hurricane is in the east. Behind you is the first summit of Pitchoff.

This is a good place to have lunch. You may want to walk a short way south of Balanced Rocks to a ledge offering a splendid view of the Cascade Lakes.

The trip can be extended on a pretty trail by continuing from the junction up to the first peak of Pitchoff Mountain. The trail narrows considerably and is quite easy. The round trip to the summit and back to the junction will add another 45 minutes and 1.1 mi. (1.8 km) to your outing. The summit elevation is 3600 ft. (1101 m).

Stagecoach Rock. A little-known monument between Lake Placid and Keene commemorates the passing of the day of the stagecoach in the Adirondacks. Some 4.6 mi. (7.5 km) east of Heart Lake Road is a boulder at a pulloff on the north side of Rt. 73. (This is just downhill from the trailhead to Cascade Mountain, across the road from Upper Cascade Lake.) Carved into the large rock are a stagecoach, team, and driver.

From 1855 to 1890, the stagecoach was the primary means of public conveyance in the mountains. The main stations were Elizabethtown, Keeseville, Ausable Forks, and North Creek. From these locations, routes spread out through the North Country to interior towns and resort hotels.

For fifteen years, Fred Cook drove six horses over the treacherous Spruce Hill Road from Elizabethtown. "Fitch" O'Brien hauled passengers up through the much-feared Wilmington Notch. Ike Roblee headed up to Blue Mountain and Long Lake from North Creek. Dozens of other skilled drivers safely carried their charges through the woods until the "iron horse" and "horseless carriage" put them to pasture.

One day in the 1930s, Donald Rogers, a district engineer working on highways, was at work when a large boulder fell to the roadside off Pitchoff Mountain. Thinking it too nice to simply push aside, he had the forethought to see a use for it. Eventually Louis Brown of Carnes Granite Co., Inc., made a sketch and Wilfred Carnes sandblasted the outline of the stagecoach and team onto the boulder. It is a fitting tribute from the highway department to a mode of transportation of another era.

ADK

Stagecoach Rock

32. Noonmark Mountain from Round Pond

Round-trip Time—5 hrs.
Round-trip Distance—6.7 mi. (10.9 km)
Elevation Change—1991 ft. (609 m)
Summit Elevation—3556 ft. (1087 m)
Difficulty—A steady climb of fair effort.
Maps—Elizabethtown and Mt. Marcy (15' quadrangles)
      Mt. Marcy and Witherbee (metric quadrangles)

Noonmark gets its name because the sun stands directly over it at noon as viewed from Keene Valley. This middle-sized peak presents a panorama of great beauty. From its bare-rock pinnacle can be seen most of the major peaks.

Access to the trailhead is the Round Pond Trail off Rt. 73. This is 1.1 mi. (1.8 km) southeast of Chapel Pond and 3.0 mi. (4.9 km) northwest of the intersection of Rts. 9 and 73. It is on the southwest side of the road. A large parking area is just north of the trailhead.

The 0.6 mi. (1.0 km) hike into Round Pond is a moderate but steady climb over a well-used route. During the ten-minute walk, you follow red DEC trail markers to the top of a grade and then drop down toward the pond. Before reaching the camping area at the water's edge, the trail turns right. It begins a level swing around the north shore of the water. This pretty section has an unusual amount of both white birch and cedars.

Pulling away from the pond, you begin a steady ascent. For the next half hour the trail changes from a moderate to a moderately steep slope, following a stream up a col on the south edge of Round Mountain. At 1.6 mi. (2.6 km) the trail levels, then descends slightly and finally levels again. A junction is reached at 2.3 mi. (3.8 km).

The blue-marked Dix Trail from St. Huberts crosses your route here. Orange ATIS (Adirondack Trail Improvement Society) trail markers take you straight ahead, up the Felix Adler Trail toward the summit of Noonmark. Moderately steep to steep grades are found on this eroded section of trail. Some interesting rock cuts are passed through.

About a half hour later, the first lookout is reached as bare rock and spruces appear. Dix Mountain and Nippletop are seen to the south. As elevation is gained, several more lookouts are passed. Soon Round Top, Giant, and Rocky Peak mountains are seen to the right, to the northeast. The trees decrease in both number and size. One last rise takes you to the bald summit. The whole High Peak Region is before you.

The emerald carpet of conifers spreads out toward the Great Range. Gothics is spectacular. Mt. Marcy is to the left of Gothics. Beyond the Great Range, Johns Brook Valley and The Brothers are seen. The Dix Range is to the south. Hunter's Pass cuts sharply between Dix Mountain and Nippletop. Spend a long time on this summit. **ADK**

81

33. The Crows Mountains

Round-trip Time—3 hrs.
Round-trip Distance—2.7 mi. (4.4 km)
Elevation Change—1220 ft. (373 m)
Summit Elevation—2800 ft. (856 m)
Difficulty—Steep but short.
Maps—Elizabethtown and Ausable Forks (15' quadrangles)
     Lake Placid and Lewis (metric quadrangles)

The joy of these two small peaks is the immense amount of open-rock climbing found here. Excellent views are available for the time expended. Take a good book and spend a long afternoon on top of the world.

Access to the trailhead is off East Hill Road from the village of Keene. The ADK trailhead is on the north side of the road, 2.1 mi. (3.4 km) from Keene. Note the mileage carefully, since the trailhead sign is on a tree just a few feet off the road. Parking is found a little farther down the road from the trailhead. The Mountain House is also 0.23 mi. (0.3 km) beyond the trail.

The trail wends its way through an open hardwood stand to a pine woods. Red ADK markers then take you on a 15-minute, steady climb to the beginning of the rocks. You pass a large boulder, a huge U-shaped rock, and an immense oak tree.

Turning right at a vertical rock face, you start angling up the side of Little Crow Mountain. The trail is now almost entirely over rock. Outlooks soon appear as you very rapidly gain elevation. Cairns and paint blazes mark much of the way. Passing below the west summit of Little Crow, you next reach the flat, easy summit.

An unmarked cairn junction is found here. It is easy to miss. Cairns lead left to a very large rock pile at 0.9 mi. (1.5 km), indicating the true summit. Summit elevation is 2540 ft. (778 m); the ascent has been 960 ft. (294 m). The cairns then lead back to the trail over to Big Crow Mountain. Had you followed the cairns to the right of the junction instead of going to the Little Crow Summit, they would have led you to this location.

Big Crow Mountain stands before you. You must carefully follow the cairns and markers as you drop down to the wooded col between the two peaks.

Steep climbing now takes you up the meandering route to the bare summit of Big Crow Mountain. It is a beautiful spot. Directly back over Little Crow, huge Cascade Mountain looms in the distance. To the left, down the valley, is Giant. Farther left, in the southeast, is Hurricane Mountain, easily located because of its fire tower. Much closer, to the north, is the Nun-da-ga-o Ridge (Soda Range).

The return trip offers many options. The reverse of the ascent is suggested if only one vehicle is available to the party. If you have a second vehicle, a most enjoyable descent can be made to the south, ending at Big Crow Clearing. The second vehicle could be left there by turning left onto O'Toole Road just past the Mountain House. The clearing is the state's trailhead for this mountain and is 1.2 mi. (1.9 km) up O'Toole Road. You can make this loop even if you don't have a second vehicle, but it means walking on a dirt road for part of the way.   **ADK**

THE LAKE PLACID & SARANAC LAKE SECTION

The Lake Placid and Saranac Lake section is distinct because it is the transition zone of the two Adirondack land divisions. To the south and east of Lake Placid lie the High Peaks of the Mountain Belt. Beyond the Saranacs to the west is the Lake Region.

It was this beautiful setting that attracted such greats as Ralph Waldo Emerson, Louis Agassiz, and William James Stillman in the mid-1800s. What fascinating conversations must have echoed across the waters at their "philosophers' camp" on Follensby Pond and later at Ampersand Pond. It took the Civil War to prevent this group from continuing its annual summer gathering.

The country is just as inviting today as it was in yesteryear. Many combine canoeing with hiking here.

34. Ampersand Mountain

Round-trip Time—4 hrs. 30 min.
Round-trip Distance—5.4 mi. (8.7 km)
Elevation Change—1775 ft. (543 m)
Summit Elevation—3352 ft. (1025 m)
Difficulty—First half is easy, second half very steep and rugged.
Maps—Santanoni (15' quadrangle)
        Ampersand Lake (metric quadrangle)

Standing on Ampersand Mountain, you can gaze into the bold face of the Seward Range and then to the more distant High Peaks. Turning around, you can look below to the Saranacs and the lake country. Such a contrast in beauty is not available to this degree anywhere else in the Adirondacks. This bald summit has long been a favorite, though you must work to earn your reward.

The trailhead is located on Rt. 3, 12 mi. (19.4 km) east of Tupper Lake and 8 mi. (13 km) south of Saranac Lake village. A large parking area is on the north side of the road, with the trailhead signpost on the south side. Dropping over the back edge of the parking area is a 0.5 mi. (0.8 km) trail leading to a lean-to on Middle Saranac Lake. This is an attractive camping location. A crescent-shaped beach of "amber sand," from which this region is thought to have gained its name, makes an after-climb swim hard to resist.

The trail begins at a barred gate. Past it, a broad path takes you along a level route through a woods having an almost park-like quality. For 20 minutes, the beauty of well-spaced hemlocks keeps your interest. A few gurgling brooks are crossed before a long section of corduroy indicates that changing terrain is ahead.

With the crossing of a shorter, second section of corduroy, moderate climbing begins. At 1.6 mi. (2.2 km), just before you arrive at the remains of the fire observer's cabin in a small clearing, the summit can be seen above the trees. Avoid the old trail that goes straight ahead across Dutton Brook at this point.

The new trail swings to the right side of the clearing and follows the creek for a way. A short section of blowdown is easily bypassed.

The last mile (1.6 km) to the summit is very rugged. Over 1300 vertical ft. (398 m) must be scaled on a poor trail. Tree roots, steep dirt sections, and a rocky stream bed demand your constant attention.

Finally, at 2.4 mi. (3.9 km), a col provides a level respite. An extremely large rock overhang is passed under. The trail circles the summit and then a short section of moderately steep grade brings you to the bare rock. Yellow painted markers lead you up the massive rock to the peak.

To your left, in the west, the Saranacs spread out before you. Middle Saranac is smallest and has several islands. Upper Saranac is behind it. Lower Saranac is to its right toward the north. Northeast is Oseetah Lake, with Scarface Mountain at its right. Haystack and McKenzie are beyond Scarface. Whiteface Mountain is still farther off to the northeast. Below you to the southeast is Ampersand Pond. Beyond the pond stands Seward Mountain and, to its left, Mt. Seymour. Imagine, if you will, a little firecracker of a man snowshoeing up Ouluska Pass between those two mountains. He is headed for Coreys on his annual visit to civilization at Christmas time. Such a man actually existed. His name was Noah John Rondeau and he did this every year for over a quarter of a century.

Closer in, to the left of Ampersand Pond, is Van Dorrien Mountain. Just over its shoulder is Algonquin, thrusting 5114 ft. (1564 m) skyward in the distance. To the south is Kempshall Mountain on Long Lake.

Yellow paint markers take you on a short distance to a slightly lower part of the summit. The foundation supports of the old fire tower can still be found here. Nearby, a bronze plate is attached to the rock. It commemorates Walter Channing Rice, "the hermit of Ampersand," who manned the tower for many, many years.

This mountain is often climbed on snowshoes in the winter, though considerable skill is needed for the last mile.   **ADK**

35. Baker Mountain

Round-trip Time—2 hrs.
Round-trip Distance—1.8 mi. (2.9 km)
Elevation Change—884 ft. (270 m)
Summit Elevation—2452 ft. (750 m)
Difficulty—Short, but steep; tough little climb.
Maps—Saranac Lake (15' quadrangle)
       Saranac Lake (metric quadrangle)

This mountain almost was not included in this guide because of its relatively short length. But what it lacks in distance, it makes up in steepness. The view is excellent.

Access to the trailhead is off Rt. 86 in Saranac Lake village. Turn right at the traffic island as you enter the village from Lake Placid. Cross the railroad tracks and turn left onto Pine Street, a dirt road. Follow Pine Street, crossing the tracks again, until you reach East Pine Street. Turn right, again crossing the tracks on an overpass. Follow the paved East Pine Street to the north end of Moody Pond. The trailhead is 0.2 mi. (0.3 km) past a small bathing area set off by a rustic fence. Parking is on the right side of the road.

The beginning of the trail is not marked. Care should be taken to follow directions. The general rule is that when there is a choice of paths to follow, take the one that shows the most use.

The trail starts up an old tote road but leaves it almost immediately. A path leads to the right, up a very short grade, to a second tote road. Turning left, walk about 100 ft. (32 m) to where the trail branches to the right at a junction. This road goes straight along a slight grade over a hardscrabble road. It soon arrives at another fork. Avoid following the road to the right, which has a posted sign on a tree. Take the left fork onto a dirt trail, which skirts the right side of an abandoned quarry. After a few yards, the trail branches to the right on a broad path. Avoid following the rim of the quarry.

Once through this short section, which only covers about 0.1 mi. (0.2 km), the way to the summit is clear. It is up. Moderately steep to steep grades take you along your way for a few minutes. Then a welcome level stretch lets you catch your breath. You are ready for the very steep part, which appears at 0.6 mi. (1.0 km).

The trail is wide and not dangerous, but take your time. It is a rather long section of steady climbing. As the trail becomes more rocky, the first red ADK trail markers are seen. Follow them carefully.

A series of lookouts give excellent views of the high peaks to the southeast. Ampersand Mountain is seen to the south, just beyond large Oseetah Lake. The summit provides a good view eastward. Haystack Mountain is seen across McKenzie Pond. The long hulk of McKenzie Mountain is close behind Haystack Mountain. A short path leads north of the summit to a cliff of considerable height. From it you can see St. Regis

Mountain, the large bulk of Debar Mountain, and a few other of the outlying peaks to the north. In all, this amazing little peak looks out to 28 major mountains.   **ADK**

---

36. Haystack Mountain

Round-trip Time—5 hrs.
Round-trip Distance—6.6 mi. (10.7 km)
Elevation Change—1240 ft. (379 m)
Summit Elevation—2878 ft. (880 m)
Difficulty—A very moderate hike, with short steep sections near end.
Maps—Saranac Lake (15' quadrangle)
       Saranac Lake (metric quadrangle)

It seems there are as many Haystack mountains in the Adirondacks as there are Mud lakes. This one is in Ray Brook, near Saranac Lake. The peak is overshadowed by huge McKenzie Mountain but offers a better view for a lot less effort. In fact, the whole trip is about as nice a day hike as anyone could ask for. The view from the top is excellent.

The old trailhead behind DEC Region 5 Headquarters in Ray Brook was moved in 1984. Today, the trailhead is at a road pulloff on Rt. 86, 1.6 mi. (2.6 km) east of the DEC Headquarters building and 1.4 mi. (2.3 km) west of the junction with Old Military Road. The trailhead has a DEC sign and blue DEC trail markers.

The trail quickly crosses a small knoll and a wet area. Swinging left, it climbs gradually over two crests before dropping to a small stream at 0.5 mi. (0.8 km).

Turning left across the creek, the route gradually gains elevation along the base of some low ledges to a point where another slight descent begins at 1.1 mi. (1.8 km). A small clearing at 1.5 mi. (2.4 km) offers viewing to the southwest. Then, at 1.8 mi. (2.9 km), the trail merges with the original trail, which comes in from the left.

The old woods road takes you up a grade beside Little Ray Brook to a junction at 2.4 mi. (3.9 km). The Haystack Mountain trail bears left, continuing on the level. Avoid the McKenzie Mountain trail, which climbs to the right.

The water-supply dam of the old State Sanatorium is soon crossed, and a half hour of step-like ascents begins. Moderately steep to steep slopes alternate with level stretches, preventing tiring. The forest you are passing through is mature maple-beech hardwood.

At 3.0 mi. (4.9 km) rather steep climbing commences; before long, you reach a rocky outlook. Painted lines take you up to the wooded summit. A large, grassy meadow provides an open vista to the east and south.

Walking downslope a short way, one can see Whiteface Mountain to the left, in the northeast. Big Burn Mountain is directly before you. To the southeast, the outline of Algonquin appears to be the largest moun-

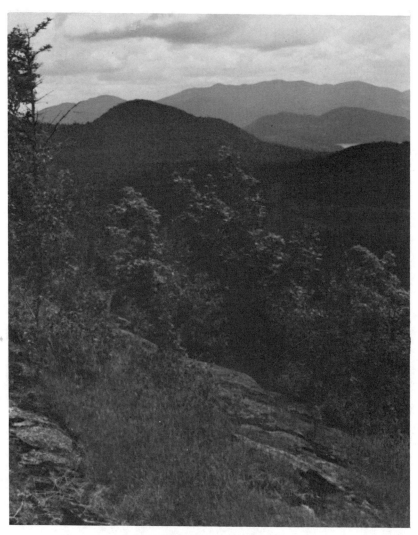

View from Haystack Mountain

tain on the horizon. Mt. Marcy is to her left, looking smaller because it is farther away. Most of the High Peaks can be seen.

Closer in, Scarface Mountain is to the right front, with what was the 1980 Olympic Village at its right. It is now a state prison. Farther south is Ampersand Mountain, distinctly separate from the more distant Seward Range at its left. On a clear day this has to be one of the most enjoyable views in the mountains.

A short walk northward through the spruces provides a lookout across the narrow valley to huge McKenzie Mountain. Both Haystack and McKenzie mountains make good winter snowshoeing outings. Haystack is shorter by 3.0 mi. (4.9 km).

ADK

37. Owen and Copperas Ponds Walk

Round-trip Time—2 hrs.
Round-trip Distance—2.6 mi. (4.1 km)
Elevation Change—174 ft. (53 m)
Difficulty—Easy with a few short grades.
Maps—Lake Placid (15' quadrangle)
　　　　Lake Placid (metric quadrangle)

　　A walk at Owen and Copperas ponds can be a two-hour interlude or a whole afternoon of relaxation in the midst of natural beauty. The route described here can be extended by a side trip to Winch Pond. If two vehicles are available, a loop route is possible by leaving the second car at the Copperas Pond trailhead, 1.0 mi. (1.6 km) north from where the Owen Pond trailhead is located on Rt. 86.

　　Access to the Owen Pond trailhead is on the east side of Rt. 86, approximately 5.0 mi. (8.1 km) northeast of the intersection of Rts. 86

OWEN AND COPPERAS PONDS

Whiteface Mountain from Copperas Pond

and 73 at Lake Placid. This is about 2.0 mi. (3.2 km) beyond the junction with River Road, which comes across from the Olympic Ski Jump on Rt. 73. There is parking for a few cars at the trailhead and also parking space on the opposite side of the road.

Blue DEC trail markers follow a tote road for about 420 ft. (129 m). The trail then turns left from the tote road and continues along the right bank of Owen Pond Brook. A small grade brings you up to a hemlock grove. You hike far above the brook, looking down at its rippling flow. Owen Pond is reached at 0.6 mi. (0.9 km). Take the time to go to one of the side paths leading to its shoreline. One of the Sentinel mountains stands out across the water at the far shore.

The path moves away from the pond, climbing a slope which alternately steepens and lessens. Swinging to the north, it reaches a junction at the top of the grade. The pond is seen below and the trail descends steeply to it at the right. Copperas Pond Lean-to No. 1 (placed on an ideal campsite) is reached at 1.3 mi. (2.1 km). An attractive picture emerges as one gazes across the pond. Great cliffs rise straight upward, with the crest of Whiteface Mountain soaring still higher beyond them as a backdrop. It is truly spectacular.

This short walk changes continuously as the seasons cast their special magic. Early spring flowers spatter the open woods floor. Young buds soon burst into leaves, drawing a veil over the forest. Shadows play their tricks and spiders weave their webs in the warming days of summer. Radiant leaves form a patchwork quilt, with conifers adding just the right amount of green, as autumn suddenly dashes in. Finally, the white snow of winter clears the easel until nature's artist begins afresh in the new year.

Soon after passing the lean-to, a trail right leads to Winch Pond. Bearing left, a second lean-to is found on the north shoreline. A path continues around the pond edge to a nice picnic and swimming spot.

The second Rt. 86 trailhead is another 0.7 mi.(1.2 km) along the trail. A second branch trail to Winch Pond is reached shortly after crossing the bridge over Copperas Pond Outlet. Should you turn right here, you will reach Winch Pond after a short 20-minute side trip over a minor ridge. By bearing left at this junction, you proceed toward Rt. 86. **ADK**

---

38. Wanika Falls

Round-trip Time—7 hrs.
Round-trip Distance—13.4 mi. (21.8 km)
Elevation Change—582 ft. (178 m)
Difficulty—A very long trip over easy terrain.
Maps—Santanoni or Saranac Lake (15' quadrangles)
　　　　Ampersand Lake (metric quadrangle)

The Wanika Falls hike is a beautiful walk over the north end of the Northville-Placid Trail. The trip is longer than it used to be because of the rerouting of this section of trail in 1977. It is a long day's hike. The trail and falls are worth the effort, however. Endurance and time are factors for consideration. The actual terrain covered is not at all difficult.

Access to the trailhead is off the Averyville Road, south of Lake Placid. Averyville Road intersects Rt. 73 in the village of Lake Placid at the Newman Opera House. If approaching Lake Placid from Saranac Lake on Rt. 86, you may take the Old Military Road to the Northville-Placid Trail at the Averyville Road intersection. Old Military Road can also be reached from Rt. 73 near the Lake Placid Horse Show grounds. From the N-P sign at the Old Military Road intersection, drive 1.2 mi. (1.9 km) south on Averyville Road to the Chubb River bridge. A N-P sign indicates the trailhead and a small parking area at this point. A much larger and better parking area is found 900 ft. (275 m) farther down the road at the right.

The trail passes a DEC register and follows blue trail markers along a tote road beside Chubb River for 475 ft. (145 m). Here, it branches left and becomes a foot path. Elevation is gradually gained. The route crosses several tributaries and low divides as it progresses generally southward in a sweeping arc. The undulating course passes through a hardwood forest on a good trail for the next 1.2 mi. (2.0 km).

The next 1.1 mi. (1.7 km) has several soggy spots that must be crossed. They are somewhat dispersed and are of no consequence.

Once past this wet section, you re-enter the hardwoods. The next 3.6 mi. (5.8 km) to Chubb River passes through some of the nicest forest in the Adirondacks. About half an hour after beginning this section, you cross a bridge and begin a long, gradual climb on an old tote road. A

Wanika Falls

gurgling brook is below you to the right. As you reach the top of the grade, the trail branches left, away from the tote road. Soon after, a rather large vlei comes into view on the right. Finally, about three hours after you began this trip, you descend a small grade and connect up with the old N-P Trail cutoff at Chubb River.

A rather bouncy bridge takes you over a high rocky section of the Chubb River. It might be well to walk upstream a short distance and rock-hop across the water where it is much safer. Turning left from the bridge, the route takes you upstream beside the river. For 0.7 mi.(1.1 km) you steadily gain elevation until the water is far below you. The trail levels and you soon reach the trail junction for Wanika Falls. Were you to continue straight ahead for another 124.5 mi. (201.7 km), you would arrive at Northville on the Great Sacandaga Lake, having passed through one of the most remote parts of the Adirondacks.

Turn left and proceed about 500 ft. (153 m) up the steep trail to the Wanika Falls lean-to. Some falls are seen here, but the really spectacular falls are found about 100 yds. (92 m) upstream from the lean-to. Here, in a series of drops, water cascades several hundred feet to a pool. It is not only beautiful but beckons you to a refreshing swim before lunch.

39. Mt. Jo

Round-trip Time—1 hr. and 45 min.
Round-trip Distance—2.3 mi. (3.7 km)
Elevation Change—710 ft. (217 m)
Summit Elevation—2876 ft. (880 m)
Difficulty—An easy mountain because of its short distance, but steep in places.
Maps—Mt. Marcy (15' quadrangle)
　　　　Keene Valley (metric quadrangle)

Mt. Jo is a special mountain. In 1877, Henry Van Hoevenberg and his fiancée Josephine Scofield climbed Mt. Marcy to choose, from all they surveyed, the place for their future home. A tiny heart-shaped lake, far to the north, was selected. The mountain near it was named Mt. Jo, after Josephine. Then tragedy struck. Josephine died within a year. She was never to see her home completed. But Van Hoevenberg carried on and completed the well-known Adirondack Lodge, which was later destroyed by the great forest fire of 1903. Some years later the Lake Placid Club acquired the property, rebuilding the inn. Melville Dewey, a driving force behind the reconstruction and a proponent of phonetic spelling, provided his own inimitable mark of peculiar spelling. Today the complex is known as Adirondak Loj and is owned and operated by the Adirondack Mountain Club. Tender memories of a time forever lost linger on this tiny mountain top.

Mt. Jo is on the Adirondak Loj property at Heart Lake. It is reached via Heart Lake Road by turning off Rt. 73 at the DEC "Trail to the High Peaks" sign. This is 4.0 mi. (6.5 km) southeast of the village of Lake Placid. At 4.8 mi. (7.8 km) down Heart Lake Road, turn left into the public parking area.

From the entrance of the parking area, walk 500 ft. (153 m) back down Heart Lake Road to the Indian Pass trail on the left. Follow this trail a short distance, turning right when a T-junction is reached. You soon cross a small bridge. The Mt. Jo trail begins on the right, immediately beyond the bridge.

The trail is well-marked with blue paint blazes and ADK markers on small stakes. Leaving the Indian Pass trail, the route immediately turns left and climbs to the junction of the Long and Short summit trails. To make a loop trip, the Long Trail is described for the ascent and the Short Trail is described for the descent.

The Long Trail bears left and gradually circles the base of the mountain, with little change of elevation. At 0.6 mi. (1.0 km), a sharp pitch begins your real climbing. At 1.0 mi. (1.6 km), the Short Trail rejoins the Long Trail. From here, the remainder of the trip is easy, with a little rock climbing just before reaching the summit.

Splendid views are found from Mt. Jo. Heart Lake is seen below. Looking southward, the MacIntyre Range of Wright Peak, Algonquin, Boundary, Iroquois, and Marshall opens up. Slightly to the left, over Mt. Colden, Mt. Marcy can be seen. Farther left, over Phelps, the Great Range comes into view. Whiteface Mountain can be seen in the northwest. All in all, this is a very fine observation point for such a short climb.

The return route is the reverse of the ascent until the junction with the Short Trail is reached. The Short Trail branches left. It is quite steep but has some rather unusual rock formations along the way. It does require a bit of agile footwork in places, since some of the trail is heavily eroded, but a number of outlooks make the paint-marked trail interesting.

Paul Smiths Visitor Interpretive Center.

This center has much of interest to the hiker in summer and to the skier and snowshoer in winter. Its purpose is to inform the visitor about the Adirondacks. Spend a day here if at all possible.   **ADK**

The Cranberry Lake, Wanakena, and West section is a relatively isolated area. The old ways still linger here. The people have a pride and friendliness that clearly tell you how much they enjoy this country.

Frederic Remington understood this when he summered at Witch's Bay on Cranberry Lake. The feelings of many others are expressed near the mouth of Sucker Brook on this same lake;, there, chiseled into a rock, are words in commemoration of a world-champion, fly-casting champion of yesteryear: "In memory of Reuben Wood, a genial gentleman and great fisherman who was fond of these solitudes." Many today are still drawn to these solitudes.

The river people along the St. Lawrence have passed Sunday Rock for years on their way to the "South Woods." It took the automobile, however, to open the way into this region from other directions. Even the rivers flow northward, away from the larger cities of the state. Now, campers from Syracuse, Rochester, and Watertown frequent the area.

For flatland hiking in an exceptional setting, this is a marvelous section of the Adirondacks. The hiker who also likes to paddle a canoe will find no finer place to combine the two pleasures.

Access to this section is by Rts. 3, 56, and 58. Towns are far apart and traffic is light. Be sure your vehicle is in proper running condition.

Sunday Rock. Four-tenths of a mile (0.6 km) north of the Raquette River bridge in the town of South Colton is a dull, grey boulder. It used to sit along the dusty road traveled by vacationers in their wagons as they headed for the "South Woods" from the Canton area. Natives have long known it as Sunday Rock.

As boulders go, it is unremarkable—rather modest in size, though a bit more regular in shape than most. Its significance is not in substance, but in what it represents.

For some reason, this rock always caught the eye of the tired traveler on his way to a place of revitalization. It was said there was no Sunday beyond this rock. Once past this point, one entered a special world of timelessness where one was freed of the restrictions of more formal society.

When the automobile came along, the narrow road had to be widened. Sunday Rock was in the way. A hue and cry arose throughout the North Country. The Sunday Rock Association was formed to save it. First the *Watertown Daily Times* and later the *Brooklyn Eagle* took up the banner.

Public opinion eventually prevailed. The rock was carefully removed from its position and today sits in its little park with dignity and respect.

The whole thing was a sentimental gesture, but typical of those who love the Adirondacks. They know Sunday Rock represents the spirit that draws them to these woods. Though the physical beauty of this land is

Sunday Rock at South Colton

immense, it is really the sense of unencumbered freedom in the midst of this beauty that is unique here. This ageless boulder symbolizes man's determination that the essence of the Adirondacks shall always survive. **ADK**

40. Cat Mountain

Round-trip Time—5 hrs.
Round-trip Distance—11.2 mi. (18.1 km)
Elevation Change—766 ft. (234 m)
Summit Elevation—2261 ft. (691 m)
Difficulty—Easy, but a fairly long trip.
Map—Cranberry Lake (15' quadrangle)

This trail is part of an immense hiking system into one of the finest wilderness areas of the Adirondacks. Extended trips of over a week are possible in this region.

Access to the trailhead is from the village of Wanakena. Wanakena is 1 mi. (1.6 km) off Rt. 3. As you proceed to Wanakena, bear right at any road forks you come to. After you cross the Oswegatchie River on a one-lane metal bridge, travel 0.5 mi. (0.8 km) until you reach a small DEC sign indicating the Dead Creek Flow fire road. There is parking just past the gated fire road.

Follow the fire road 2.0 mi. (3.2 km) to its end. The almost-level, grassy lane passes through a most interesting deciduous forest. After about 25 minutes of walking, you pass a pretty little vlei on the right. Five minutes later, you catch your first glimpse of Dead Creek Flow on the left. The fire road then parallels the flow until you reach its terminus. Here, you'll find a picnic table and a fireplace. Janack's Landing can be seen across the water.

The trail, now a path, continues on another 1.1 mi. (1.8 km) to another trail junction. On the way, Dead Creek and a second brook are crossed on log bridges. From the junction, Janack's Landing is 0.2 mi. (0.3 km) to the left. This makes a good swimming spot on the return trip.

Bearing right, you are led by red markers on a flat trail for some 15 minutes. Then you very gradually gain elevation as you pass through a draw. Approaching the end of the draw, the trail becomes a moderately steep grade for a short distance.

Just beyond the height of land, you again come to a trail junction. The blue Plains Trail goes straight on down the slope ahead. Stay on the red trail, which bears left along the ridge.

Moving on, you soon hear the sound of rushing water. Before long, you reach the cascading waters of Glasby Pond Outlet. The trail follows the outlet a short half mile (0.8 km) to Glasby Pond. A pretty fern meadow is passed through just before you reach the pond. At the pond's edge you cross the outlet on a log bridge. Glasby Pond is a jewel. Its dark water is surrounded by bushes, giving it a primitive look.

The red trail soon bears right and for some distance is above the water level, providing a splendid view of the pond and the mountain beyond.

Cat Mountain Pond from Cat Mountain

Leaving the pond, the trail begins to climb gradually until a trail junction is reached. The yellow trail to the right leads to Cowhorn Junction. Continue straight ahead for Cat Mountain.

The summit is only 0.6 mi. (0.8 km) ahead. The trail is moderate and levels frequently. Eventually you run straight into a very high massive bluff. The only
real climbing occurs here as you climb a very steep 100 vertical feet up a narrow rock path.

At the top the trail swings right, passes a couple lookouts, and soon reaches the summit. Only the foundation of the fire tower remains, but you have a splendid view from the open rock. As you move around the rock bluff to the left, charming vistas appear to the east, where the high peaks are seen in the far distance. Cat Mt. Pond is seen below.

As your eyes sweep the vast forest region, it is hard to believe that all this was desolation in 1908, when sparks from locomotives started fires that devastated the region. The recuperative power of nature is great, but let's hope that man has not forgotten this terrible lesson from our past. **ADK**

41. High Falls

Round-trip Time—5 hrs. 30 min.
Round-trip Distance—12.8 mi. (20.7 km)
Elevation Change—123 ft. (38 m)
Difficulty—Easy walking, but a long trip.
Map—Cranberry Lake (15' quadrangle)

High Falls is a cataract on the Oswegatchie River, where the flow squeezes through a narrow channel in the rock and jets out in a burst of white foam. Cascading downward, its cooling spray sets up breezes that make this a tremendously pleasant place to be on a hot summer day.

Access to the trailhead is from the village of Wanakena. Wanakena is 1.0 mi. (1.6 km) off Rt. 3. As you proceed to Wanakena, bear right at any road forks you come to. When you cross the Oswegatchie River on a one-lane metal bridge, take care. At 0.1 mi. (0.2 km) beyond the bridge on the right is a small sign pointing down the High Falls truck road. The trail begins at a metal gate a few hundred feet along this road.

Parking is available on the right side of the paved road, just beyond the tennis courts and past the turn-off for the truck road. Parking also is available for a small fee at the private home just before the truck trail gate.

The first part of the DEC red-marked trail is perfectly flat and open. You pass a narrow pond on the left and finally begin to climb gradually upward as you enter the woods. Below on the right, Skate Creek can be seen. The trail becomes quite rocky and reaches the junction with the Leary Trail at 1.8 mi. (2.9 km).

Follow the blue-marked trail, which branches left and proceeds up a fair grade. Over the next 3.0 mi. (4.9 km) the trail rises moderately and drops frequently as it takes you through a deciduous forest. A few swampy areas and streams are crossed. Beaver activity may cause minor walking difficulty just before the trail emerges from the forest onto the trail.

Leave the blue trail you have been following. It continues straight into the distant Five Ponds Wilderness Area. Instead, turn left and follow the red-marked truck trail. High Falls is another 1.6 mi. (2.6 km).

This portion of the truck trail is both easier to walk on and more interesting in its surroundings than the previous portion. The soil is sandier. Tamarack trees, the only deciduous conifers, are seen in this section. Their delicate stringy boughs are easily spotted.

About a mile (1.6 km) down this road the Plains Trail comes in from the left. If time permits on the return trip, you might follow it in a ways. It is a most unique place. The extensive open region of berry bushes and flowers doesn't seem to grow in with trees. Extreme variations in yearly groundwater levels might be the reason. On any account, a walk through the Plains is an unforgettable experience.

Eight-tenths of a mile (1.3 km) farther on you'll arrive at High Falls.

A lean-to is located on each side of the river. An attractive wooden bridge crosses the stream above the falls. Deep pools invite you to swim. Enjoy yourself. **ADK**

High Falls on Oswegatchie River

42. The Moore Trail

Round-trip Time—2 hrs.
Round-trip Distance—4 mi. (6.5 km)
Elevation Change—Negligible
Difficulty—Easy.
Map—Cranberry Lake (15' quadrangle)

The Moore Trail is a pretty walk along the north shoreline of the Oswegatchie River from Wanakena to Inlet.

Access to the trailhead is from the village of Wanakena. Wanakena is 1.0 mi. (1.6 km) off Rt. 3. As you proceed to Wanakena, bear right at any forks you come to. Just before the single-lane metal bridge across the Oswegatchie River, you notice a small DEC sign attached to a tree on the right. It indicates the direction to Inlet and is marked 2.0 mi. (3.2 km). This is the Moore Trail. You may park your car off the road at this point. The wide, grassy lane for canoe access leads directly to the stream. A short distance along this way, you'll notice a narrow trail to the right through the tall grass. Follow this. It very soon becomes a wide and pretty woods trail along the river.

The trail is essentially level except for a few places where it briefly rises a few feet above water level. It follows the stream to Inlet. This section of the river moves rapidly and has many rocks. It is not passable by canoeists unless they are whitewater experts. Even then some portages are required.

On a summer day, the trail provides a pleasant respite for the traveler. Many places beckon you to sit at the shoreline to watch the surging water. Its constant roar masks most other sounds and is relaxing. It is an excellent place to practice photography.   **ADK**

View from the Moore Trail

WANAKENA TRAILS

Wanakena Channel

Moore Trail

Wanakena

Inlet

Dead Creek Flow

Janacks Landing

Cat Mt

Oswegatchie River

Leary Trail

Plains Trail

High Falls

---

43. Bear Mountain

Round-trip Time—2 hrs.
Round-trip Distance—3.6 mi. (5.8 km)
Elevation Change—742 ft. (227 m)
Summit Elevation—2242 ft. (686 m)
Difficulty—Easy, with a few steep places.
Map—Cranberry Lake (15' quadrangle)

Bear Mountain is on the north shore of Cranberry Lake and offers a pretty view of the lake. Short enough so that swimming and picnicking can be combined with the climb, it makes a nice little outing.

Access to the trailhead is off Rt. 3 at the Cranberry Lake Public Campsite and Picnic Area. This is just east of the village of Cranberry Lake. Turning at the large sign, drive 1.2 mi. (1.9 km) until you come to the park's toll booth. There is a small day-use charge for entering the park. Proceed past the picnic and beach area until at 0.5 mi. (0.8 km) you reach the DEC sign for Bear Mountain. There is a large parking area at the left.

The trail leaves the right rear of the parking area where there is a trail register. Follow red DEC markers. The almost level trail passes through a predominantly beech forest. Quite rocky at first, it becomes more comfortable as elevation is gained.

Two small brooks are crossed. At 0.6 mi. (1.0 km) the grade becomes moderately steep and climbs steadily for a few moments. A short distance from where the trail briefly levels again a lean-to is passed on the left.

After crossing a small brook on a log bridge, the trail again becomes moderate to moderately steep. Soon it swings up to the left and steepens considerably. This is the only really steep part of the trail. You soon reach the top of the mountain ridge and proceed along the flat summit for about 10 minutes.

Here the forest is more open and the trees are somewhat smaller. You actually are slowly losing some elevation. Passing between two immense boulders, you enter an interesting boulder field. Strewn about like so many checkers, the many boulders in this location were dropped by the last glaciers about 10,000 years ago.

The easy walking continues, until at 1.5 mi. (2.4 km) you reach the lookout. From this point you look directly down on Joe Indian Island in Cranberry Lake. To the left is Buck Island. Beyond it at Barber's Point is the Cranberry Lake Biological Station. Run by the forestry school of Syracuse University, it provides remarkable training for future foresters. Just to the right of Joe Indian Island, Dead Creek Flow and the Wanakena Channel begin.

In 1908, fire swept this mountain top. Still earlier, a hunter who was stung by hornets got even by burning their nest and half of the mountain. He was smart enough to keep that a secret for many years.

A loop can be made by continuing along the ridge. It is a very nice trail for 0.9 mi. (1.5 km), but it does mean 1.0 mi. (1.6 km) of walking the paved road back through the park to your starting point after you leave the forest.

Still following the red DEC markers, the trail follows the ridge for a few minutes. Then it descends rather steeply for about five minutes. Moderating, the trail continues through a nice hardwood forest. A very large rock outcrop is passed on the right, at 2.4 mi. (3.4 km). Finally the lake is seen ahead through the trees. After crossing a small tributary of the lake on a rustic bridge, you reach the paved road.

Turn right and follow this road to the first junction. Turn right again and stay on this road until you reach the parking area where you left your vehicle. It will take about 20 minutes of walking to cover this distance.   **ADK**

44. Arab Mountain

Round-trip Time—1 hr. 30 min.
Round-trip Distance—2.1 mi. (3.4 km)
Elevation Change—760 ft. (232 m)
Summit Elevation—2545 ft. (778 m)
Difficulty—Easy, with varying grades.
Maps—Tupper Lake (15' quadrangle)
          Piercefield (metric quadrangle)

Geographically, this mountain sits like a large strawberry at the bottom of an enormous flattened bowl, waiting to provide a delicious dessert for the hiker. Though not great in elevation, it is higher than its immediate surroundings. There are excellent views in all directions from its summit.

Access to the trailhead is off Rt. 3. Between the hamlets of Gale and Piercefield, turn south at the sign for Conifer. At 1.7 mi. (2.8 km) there is a left turn. A large sign points the way to Eagle Crag Lake. A smaller DEC sign indicates it is 1.7 mi. (2.8 km) to Mt. Arab. It is, but that includes the walking. The trailhead is actually only 0.9 mi. (1.5 km) farther. A railroad track is crossed 0.3 mi. (0.5 km) before the small DEC sign indicating the trailhead. It is on the left side of the road. Parking is available for several cars on the opposite side of the road.

Red DEC markers lead the way through a beech-maple forest. A well-designed new trail has replaced the older one. The two criss-cross each other frequently; follow the red markers. The trail rises slowly, leveling off frequently.

At 0.4 mi. (0.6 km) a sign indicates a spring to the left. Yellow painted tree blazes lead down the slope some distance to the spring.

Soon after, the trail becomes moderately steep. It turns left at a large boulder. Reaching the ridge line at 0.6 mi. (1.0 km), the now nearly level path leads through a pretty maple and red-spruce growth. It is quite pleasant after the climbing you've just completed. Two rock outcrops are passed. The trail swings to the right around the second of these. One last rise brings you to the fire observer's cabin and the fire tower. The true summit is slightly farther on, beyond a small col, but the described trail terminates at the tower.

The summit is relatively flat. It is a floral bouquet bordered by berry bushes. To the west is Tupper Lake. Beyond the lake are the high peaks. There is a 360-degree panorama. Mt. Arab Lake and Eagle Crag Lake are below to the southeast. To the north are Mt. Matumbla and St. Regis Mountain. The rim of the horizon is full of mountain ridges.

The grades found on this trail are ideal for snowshoeing. The reward for a sunny winter's tramp to this summit would be great for such a short climb. **ADK**

The North–Northeast section has a somewhat different character from the rest of the Adirondacks. Lake Champlain dominates. The French influence is felt in its people and in the names of such places as the Ausable and Boquet rivers. The heyday of this region was founded on the steamboat, the railroad, and the stagecoach.

Ausable Forks was a primary point of embarkation for stages heading into the high peaks. At one time, the Franklin House in Franklin Falls counted well over a thousand guests each season. This was the gateway to the mountains until the automobile changed travel patterns of vacationers. Now both the stagecoach and the Franklin House have disappeared from the region.

The North-Northeast section has quietly withdrawn from the spotlight, but it still retains its own charm. It is an interesting place historically for the hiker who realizes that a knowledge of the past greatly enhances appreciation of the present. Access to this section is via I-87 (Adirondack Northway) and Rts. 30, 72, 3 and 9.

45. Poke-O-Moonshine Mountain

Round-trip Time—2 hrs. 30 min.
Round-trip Distance—2.4 mi. (3.9 km)
Elevation Change—1280 ft. (391 m)
Summit Elevation—2180 ft. (667 m)
Difficulty—A short hike, with some steep sections.
Maps—Ausable Forks (15' quadrangle)
      Lewis (metric quadrangle)

The historian Beauchamp believed the unusual name Poke-O-Moonshine was derived from the Algonquin words *Pohquis* (it is broken) and *Moosie* (smooth). *Pohquis-Moosie* described the sheer cliffs found on this mountain. Others feel the name simply refers to the haunting glens and supposed spirits of this peak. Whatever the facts, this climb rewards the hiker with outstanding views of Lake Champlain to the east and the high peaks to the southwest. In season, a profusion of ferns borders the hiking trail near the summit.

The trail begins at the south end of the Poke-O-Moonshine State Campsite along Rt. 9, about 12 mi. (19.4 km) north of Elizabethtown and 7 mi. (11.3 km) south from Keeseville. If driving north on I-87, exit at Exit 32 and drive west to Rt. 9. Take Rt. 9 north 9 mi. (15 km) to the campsite. If driving south on I-87, exit at Exit 33. Drive a short distance to Rt. 9 and then proceed southward about 3 mi. (3.9 km) to the campsite.

The red-marked DEC trail begins at the south end of the campsite. A small day-use fee will be levied for parking.

The route soon steepens, and a very high rock formation is reached. Passing it to the left, you come to outlooks after a few more minutes. The last outlook has a bench-shaped boulder that appears to have been put there especially for hikers to rest on.

The difficulty in climbing varies considerably over the next half mile (0.8 km). The glen containing the remains of the fire observer's cabin is quite picturesque and provides welcome respite. A lean-to is found on a side trail to the left of the cabin, some 65 yds. (60 m) away. A tote road beyond the lean-to has many blueberries. This is a good place to rest before the final burst to the summit.

Looking south from Poke-O-Moonshine

There are two ways to the top from the cabin. The short way makes a sharp right turn from the cabin. It leads steeply up the old eroded trial to the tower. An enclosed spring is found a few yards along this route.

The easier and now official route follows red trial markers from the right rear of the cabin. It circles the summit, gradually reaching the fire tower. Many bare ledges are passed along the way. The bare rock summit and its fire tower offer a striking panorama. To the east a sweeping view of Lake Champlain, some 8 mi. (13 km) away, stands out. The Green Mountains of Vermont form a backdrop. Mansfield and Camel's Hump are clearly seen. To the south is Deerfield Mountain, with the Jays behind it. To its left is Hurricane Mountain. Distant Gothics is on Hurricane's right shoulder. To the left of Hurricane Mountain is Giant. Right of Deerfield Mountain is the Sentinel Range, 20 miles away. Whiteface Mountain is almost due west. Lyon Mountain is due north, beyond Baldface, which is farther down the ridge. On a clear day, Mt. Royal, 90 miles off in Montreal, can be seen. The hiker who has the time can spend it well by hiking along the crest of this mountain.

Colvin surveyed from this mountain in the 1870s. The careful searcher may locate a copper bolt indicating this was Station 26 of the survey.　　　　　　　　　　　　　　　　　　　　　　　　　**ADK**

46. Lyon Mountain

Round-trip Time—3 hrs. 30 min.
Round-trip Distance—5.0 mi. (8.1 km)
Elevation Change—1790 ft. (547 m)
Summit Elevation—3830 ft. (1171 m)
Difficulty—Steep for much of the climb, a rigorous High Peak-type trail.
Map—Lyon Mountain (15' quadrangle)

Charles Merril was only eighteen in the spring of 1881 when his father sent him up Lyon Mountain. The Rev. Thomas Cook of Troy was suffering from asthma, and it was felt the high elevation might help him; young Merril was his guide. Dozens of mountains could be seen in all directions. On June 20, 1881, a roaring hail and snow storm took them by surprise and they didn't come down for two weeks. It was an exciting adventure, and Merril never forgot it. He went on to become a well-known Adirondack guide.

Access to the trailhead is off Chazy Lake Road on the southwest shore of the lake. This can be reached from Rt. 3, starting at the Chazy Lake Road sign for Lyon Mountain Village at Pickett's Corners. After passing a crossroads, turn left at the T-intersection 0.6 mi. (1.0 km) from Rt. 3. This is County Rt. 8. Continue along this route and turn right at a cross-roads after another 1.9 mi. (3.1 km). You then proceed, still on Rt. 8, for another 5.7 mi. (9.2 km) to a gravel road at the left. This once was the entry road to the former Lowenberg Ski Area. If you are approaching on Rt. 374 from Dannemora, this gravel road would be 1.8 mi. (2.9 km) south from where you pick up Rt. 8.

Proceed along this wide gravel road for 0.9 mi. (1.5 km) until you reach the ruins of the ski lodge. A large parking area is at this point. Distances in the description from this point on are estimated.

On the left side of the lodge is a hardscrabble road. It is grown in at its beginning but soon opens up. Gradually climbing, you follow this road for about a mile (1.6 km). You can see the fire tower occasionally as you walk along.

After about half an hour the road swings abruptly to the right, but your trail continues straight ahead into the woods. A small stream is soon crossed. The trail now becomes moderately steep and will remain so for another 25 minutes.

The telephone wires you have been following bring you to a small sloped clearing, where you will find the fire observer's cabin and a few outbuildings. There is a brook to the left of the cabin. The trail also goes to the left. It would be well to rest here before tackling the next stretch.

The way steepens considerably for the next three-quarters of a mile (1.2 km). It is rocky and you must watch your footing. Eventually, you'll notice a small bench at a turn in the trail. An outlook is on the right and the trail goes to the left.

From this point, the path almost levels. It takes you through a nice spruce stand. Ten minutes later the tower is before you. The rocky summit has good views. On a clear day you can see the glittering spires of Notre Dame Cathedral in Montreal. Mt. Marcy and the High Peaks are to the south. Northeast of you, Chazy Lake stretches forth. Upper and Lower Chateaugay Lakes are west. By careful observation, it is possible to trace the flow of the Saranac River almost all the way to Lake Champlain. **ADK**

47. Taylor Pond Primitive Camping Area

Maps—Lyon Mountain (15' quadrangle)
Wilmington (metric quadrangle)

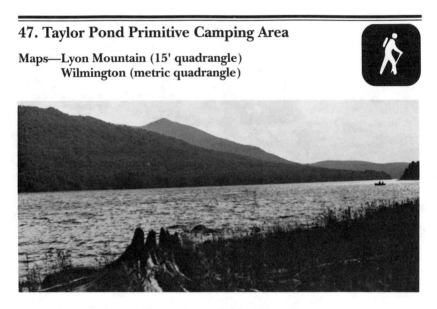

Taylor Pond Primitive Campsite

A primitive camping area is a place where camping is permitted but where facilities are kept to a minimum. Unlike the state's public campsites (state parks), there are no showers, lifeguards, or paved roads. On the other hand, there is a ranger nearby and there are a few other people.

Taylor Pond is located along the Clayburg-Ausable Forks road. It is approximately 2 mi. (3.2 km) east of the Union Falls Road, near Silver Lake. For the beginner, it offers a chance to test outdoors skills in a relatively safe atmosphere. For the experienced camper, it is a chance to enjoy the out-of-doors without the usual hardships. There are day-use and overnight camping fees.

The Taylor Pond area is truly a beautiful place, looking out toward Catamount Mountain. Over 14 mi. (22.7 km) of trails circuit the body of water. Originally developed as snowmobile trails, they are now receiving considerable winter use by cross-country skiers. In the summer they make excellent flatland hiking, often bordering the water. Day trips can be planned to meet the capabilities of the hikers.

The three lean-tos on the pond can best be reached by canoe. A few other sandy beach areas are suitable for camping.

Taylor Pond makes a good base area for more rigorous mountain activities. Catamount Mountain is just across the lake. Duncan Mountain is not far. The Silver Lake Mountain trail is again open for use.

This type of setting is fine for family and other small-group activities. The beginner who is hesitant to plunge into the forest for the first time may find the primitive camping area a happy middle ground.   **ADK**

Stump at Taylor Pond

48. Azure Mountain (Blue Mountain)

Round-trip Time—1 hr. 30 min.
Round-trip Distance—1.0 mi. (1.6 km)
Elevation Change—Estimated 700 ft. (214 m)
Summit Elevation—2518 ft. (770 m)
Difficulty—Easy, with some steep spots.
Map—Santa Clara (15' quadrangle)

Another of the outpost mountains, Azure Mountain provides a magnificent view of the distant high peaks from the north. This is in sharp contrast to the numerous small bodies of water found at its base. Altogether one earns a striking picture from climbing this small peak. Access to the trailhead is off Rt. 458, 4 mi. (6.5 km) south of St. Regis Falls or about 3 mi. (4.9 km) north of Santa Clara. At this point, Blue Mountain Road is reached on the south side of the road. It is directly opposite the Blue Mountain Inn. Blue Mountain Road is a broad gravel road in excellent condition.

Follow Blue Mountain Road for 6.7 mi. (10.9 km) to a sign on the right indicating a spring on state land. Farther on, 0.4 mi. (0.6 km), a small road is reached on the right.

This narrow dirt road leads 0.1 mi. (0.2 km) to a gate and trailhead. The trail leads another 0.3 mi. (0.5 km) to a fire observer's cabin.

The trail passes between the cabin and its outbuildings. (This used to be the starting point of the hike before the gate was installed.) As you climb, note the changing tree types as subtle ecological conditions occur.

Entering a mature maple forest, the first few hundred feet of path rise gradually. Almost all of the rest of the trail, however, varies from moderately steep to steep. It is a short but rigorous climb. The trail is marked with both red DEC markers and yellow paint blazes. To ease the ascent, numerous switchbacks have been built into the trail. For your walking safety and to prevent erosion of the mountain, follow the official trail. Do not use the goat paths that follow the telephone wires. At 0.2 mi. (0.3 km) a small sign on the right points the way to a switchback around a particularly steep spot.

The trail moderates for the last few hundred feet. The tower is soon seen ahead. Walking through high brush and long grass, you are at the tower before you can see far into the distance.

Beyond the tower open rock provides an exquisite panorama. Below you are numerous ponds. The deep blue bodies of water seem to be surrounded by a hundred shades of green.

Out to the south are Whiteface, Giant, the Great Range, Marcy, the McIntyres, and the Sewards. Closer in are dozens of lesser ridges. Huge Debar Mountain stands out in the east. The thin ribbon of water to the north is the St. Lawrence River.

The huge boulder on the edge of the drop-off on the west side of the open rock is another of nature's mysteries. Why did the glaciers of the last ice age choose that spot to leave such a giant rock? Perhaps it is to remind us of the great power of their forces. **ADK**

View from Azure Mountain

49. Debar Mountain

Round-trip Time—4 hrs. 30 min.
Round-trip Distance—7.3 mi. (11.9 km)
Elevation Change—1726 ft. (528 m)
Summit Elevation—3300 ft. (1009 m)
Difficulty—Generally easy, but the last half mile is as steep as anything in the Adirondacks that has a trail.
Map—Loon Lake and Santa Clara (15' quadrangles)

Far to the north, Debar Mountain sits beside beautiful Meacham Lake. Surrounded by state forests, she is isolated. Rising 800 ft. (245 m) in the last 0.5 mi. (0.8 km), the peak offers a mixture of easy woods walking and rugged climbing. Plan to make use of the wonderful beach at Meacham Lake.

Access to the mountain trail is from Rt. 30 at Meacham Lake Public Campsite, 18 mi. (29.2 km) south of Malone. It is 2.4 mi. (3.9 km) from the Rt. 30 park sign to the toll booth at the park. A small day-use charge is required to enter the campsite.

Proceed straight ahead from the toll booth 0.2 mi. (0.3 km) until you see a small sign on the left indicating the turn for Debar Mountain. This is the left-hand turn for Campsites 21–52. Just past Campsite 48, bear right onto the sandy road which branches off. At 0.4 mi. (0.6 km) along this road, you'll arrive at a large parking area and the gate which marks the beginning of the trail.

Red trail markers take you along a woods road through a mixed forest occasionally heavy with balsam fir. The way is almost flat in this section. At 0.8 mi. (1.3 km) bear right at the fork in the road; at 0.9 mi. (1.5 km) turn left at the junction. A small Debar Mountain trail sign high in a tree points the way.

From here the grade varies from gradual to moderately steep. In general, it steepens gradually as you progress. At 2.3 mi. (3.8 km) it would appear the trail will take you right into a boulder, but it swings to the left and continues on to a height of land at 2.5 mi. (4.0 km).

The level stretch soon ends and the trail descends slightly to a small creek. It then resumes its gradual upgrade course. A lean-to, on the left, is passed at 2.9 mi. (47 km). Your objective can be seen to the right front from this location. Soon after, the remains of the burnt-out fire observer's cabin are reached. Its small clearing is growing in from disuse.

The long walk to this point has been relatively easy; from here on, care must be taken. The trail narrows and becomes a rocky path. Before long the way becomes very steep, and it is frequently necessary to use your hands to get over some of the rocks. Eventually the trail moderates, and for the last five minutes you can catch your breath as you stride through a sweet-smelling stand of balsam fir.

Circling the base of the bald rock holding the fire tower, you finally reach the small, open, and rocky summit. The tower is not in good condition and should not be climbed.

Meacham Lake dominates the scene. Clear Pond is to its right. Far to the right is Deer River Flow. The High Peaks are to your extreme left, in the southeast. Whiteface, St. Regis, Morris, and Ampersand mountains can be spotted. Azure, Loon Lake Mountain, and Lyon Mountain are to the north.

Portions of the trail and much of the park seem ideal for cross-country skiing. The upper stretches of the trail would require some mountain-skiing skill and perhaps would be best done on snowshoes. Only those with considerable experience should try to snowshoe beyond the lean-to.   **ADK**

---

50. St. Regis Mountain

Round-trip Time—3 hrs. 30 min.
Round-trip Distance—4.9 mi. (7.9 km)
Elevation Change—1253 ft. (383 m)
Summit Elevation—2865 ft. (876 m)
Difficulty—Generally moderate, but rather steep for last part.
Maps—St. Regis (15' quadrangle)
        St. Regis Mountain (metric quadrangle)

St. Regis Mountain stands alone, surrounded by over one hundred bodies of water. The sight of these rivers, ponds, and lakes from the summit is unmatched in the Adirondacks. To the southeast, most of the high peaks can be seen on the horizon. This peak is worth scaling.

Access to the trailhead is from Keese Mills Road, near the intersection of Rts. 30 and 192 at Paul Smiths. Drive down Keese Mills Road 2.6 mi. (4.2 km). At that point, a small DEC sign for St. Regis Mountain points the way to the left at an easily missed intersection. This is just past the Canoe Carry Parking Area for Black Pond. A narrow paved road leads 0.5 mi. (0.8 km) southward to the state's locked gate across the road. At the right is a large parking area and the trail sign.

The first 0.7 mi. (1.1 km) of the red DEC-marked trail climbs over two small ridges having moderately steep grades. Take the left fork just past the top of the first ridge. Descend the second ridge and follow a metal link fence for a short distance. Crossing a dirt road, you come to what used to be the trailhead. The quality of the trail greatly improves from this point onward.

The trail levels for the next five minutes. Two swampy creeks are traversed on wooden bridges. A long moderate grade takes you along the telephone line toward the summit. This is a very nice section of trail.

About 45 minutes after your start, you pass a small cabin on the right, a stream, and the fire observer's cabin, which is up on a slope to the left. The grade now increases slightly but is still very moderate.

Log steps are reached at 1.8 mi. (2.9 km). A sign points to the left, up a moderately steep to steep grade. The slope soon moderates again until another sign is reached 15 minutes later.

The new trail rises steeply to the right front. The older, now abandoned, trail branches off to the right at a more gentle grade. The newer route is short but climbs 775 vertical ft. (237 m) in the next 0.4 mi. (0.6 km).

You will finally break out of the trees onto the open rock near the summit. Flowers and shrubs abound. Views open to the east, behind you. You soon reach the fire tower and register.

Overzealous survey crews burned off the top of St. Regis Mountain back in 1876. The bare summit offers unrestricted views in all directions. The myriad ponds and lakes are impossible to describe in detail. Upper St. Regis Lake and Spitfire Lake are due east. Lake Clear, Little Clear Pond, St. Regis Pond, and Hoel Pond are the close-by bodies of water to the south. Farther south, Upper Saranac Lake stretches out into the distance. Whiteface Mountain lies 21 mi. (34 km) away, in line with Upper St. Regis Lake. Loon Lake Mountain stands out in the northeast, beyond Black Pond. Sable and Baldface mountains separate it from the huge bulk of Debar Mountain to its left. Far in the southwest, Mt. Morris is seen to the left of Tupper Lake. The whole of the High Peaks are to the southeast. Marcy is seen in line with the right edge of Lake Clear on the horizon. Big Slide Mountain is over the center of Clear Pond. The rest of the high peaks can be picked out and identified.

This would seem to be a perfect mountain to snowshoe in the winter. The grades are moderate, except at the end. All but the summit is protected from the wind by trees. **ADK**

Glossary

Bushwhack   To make one's way through bushes or undergrowth.

Cairn   A pile of stones set up to mark a summit or route.

Col   A pass between two adjacent peaks.

Corduroy   A road, trail or bridge formed by logs laid side by side transversely to facilitate crossing swampy places.

Duff   Partly decayed vegetable matter on the forest floor.

Hardscrabble   A very rough dirt road made up largely of rocks and small stones.

Lean-to   An open camp with overhanging roof on the open side.

Massif   A large, rocky prominence.

Paint Blazes   Trail indicators painted on trees or rocks.

Tote Road   An inferior road used for hauling, such as a lumber road, often with corduroys.

Vlei   A marsh or swampy meadow (pronounced *vly*).

Index

Listings are entered by proper name first. Words like mount, mountain, lake, etc. follow the proper name.

118

Index of People

Notes

Notes

Notes

Notes

Notes

Notes

Notes

The **ADK** Forest Preserve Series

Compact, durable, hiker-oriented guides recognized as the source of Adirondack backcountry information.

1. High Peaks
2. Northern
3. Central
4. Northville-Placid Trail
5. West-Central
6. Eastern
7. Southern

Each guide contains a 33" x 20" topo map.

Available in bookstores and outdoor equipment stores or from the
Adirondack Mountain Club, R.R. 3, Box 3055, Lake George, NY 12845-9523
(518) 668-4447